Scarecrow Studies in Young Adult Literature

Series Editor: Patty Campbell

Scarecrow Studies in Young Adult Literature is intended to continue the body of critical writing established in Twayne's Young Adult Authors Series and to expand it beyond single-author studies to explorations of genres, multicultural writing, and controversial issues in young adult (YA) reading. Many of the contributing authors of the series are among the leading scholars and critics of adolescent literature, and some are YA novelists themselves.

The series is shaped by its editor, Patty Campbell, who is a renowned authority in the field, with a thirty-year background as critic, lecturer, librarian, and teacher of YA literature. Patty Campbell was the 2001 winner of the ALAN Award, given by the Assembly on Adolescent Literature of the National Council of Teachers of English for distinguished contribution to YA literature. In 1989 she was the winner of the American Library Association's Grolier Award for distinguished service to young adults and reading.

1. *What's So Scary about R. L. Stine?* by Patrick Jones, 1998.
2. *Ann Rinaldi: Historian and Storyteller*, by Jeanne M. McGlinn, 2000.
3. *Norma Fox Mazer: A Writer's World*, by Arthea J. S. Reed, 2000.
4. *Exploding the Myths: The Truth about Teens and Reading*, by Marc Aronson, 2001.
5. *The Agony and the Eggplant: Daniel Pinkwater's Heroic Struggles in the Name of YA Literature*, by Walter Hogan, 2001.
6. *Caroline Cooney: Faith and Fiction*, by Pamela Sissi Carroll, 2001.
7. *Declarations of Independence: Empowered Girls in Young Adult Literature, 1990–2001*, by Joanne Brown and Nancy St. Clair, 2002.
8. *Lost Masterworks of Young Adult Literature*, by Connie S. Zitlow, 2002.
9. *Beyond the Pale: New Essays for a New Era*, by Marc Aronson, 2003.
10. *Orson Scott Card: Writer of the Terrible Choice*, by Edith S. Tyson, 2003.
11. *Jacqueline Woodson: "The Real Thing,"* by Lois Thomas Stover, 2003.
12. *Virginia Euwer Wolff: Capturing the Music of Young Voices*, by Suzanne Elizabeth Reid, 2003.
13. *More Than a Game: Sports Literature for Young Adults*, Chris Crowe, 2004.

Janet McDonald

The Original Project Girl

Catherine Ross-Stroud

Scarecrow Studies in Young Adult Literature No. 28

THE SCARECROW PRESS, INC.
Lanham, Maryland • Toronto • Plymouth, UK
2009

SCARECROW PRESS, INC.

Published in the United States of America
by Scarecrow Press, Inc.
A wholly owned subsidiary of
The Rowman & Littlefield Publishing Group, Inc.
4501 Forbes Boulevard, Suite 200, Lanham, Maryland 20706
www.scarecrowpress.com

Estover Road
Plymouth PL6 7PY
United Kingdom

Distributed by National Book Network

British Library Cataloguing in Publication Information Available

Library of Congress Cataloging-in-Publication Data

Ross-Stroud, Catherine.
  Janet McDonald : the original project girl / Catherine Ross-Stroud.
    p. cm. — (Scarecrow studies in young adult literature ; no. 28)
  ISBN-13: 978-0-8108-5802-2 (cloth : alk. paper)
  ISBN-10: 0-8108-5802-9 (cloth : alk. paper)
  ISBN-13: 978-0-8108-6356-9 (electronic)
  ISBN-10: 0-8108-6356-1 (electronic)
  1. McDonald, Janet, 1953– 2. Authors, American—20th century—Biography.
3. African American women authors—Biography. I. Title.
  PS3563.A2789Z87 2009
  813'.54—dc22 [B]   2008030712

∞ ™ The paper used in this publication meets the minimum requirements of
American National Standard for Information Sciences—Permanence of Paper
for Printed Library Materials, ANSI/NISO Z39.48-1992.
Manufactured in the United States of America.

Janet, age 6

Contents

~

Chronology

1980 Transfers to New York University Law School
1982 Is expelled from New York University Law School; enlists in U.S. Army; becomes a member of MENSA
1984 Applies and is accepted by Columbia University Journalism School; is honorably discharged from the Army after Army officials learn of her trouble at NYU; completes journalism degree at Columbia; works as summer intern at Agence France-Presse in Paris; is readmitted to NYU Law School
1985 Named senior note and comment editor to *Review of Law and Social Change*, a law journal at NYU School of Law
1986 Graduates from NYU Law School; passes New York State Bar Exam; lands a job as a legal associate at a Manhattan law firm
1989 Relocates to Seattle, Washington, and accepts a position as an associate at a corporate law firm
1991 Moves to Paris and accepts an internship in international law at a French firm
1993 Moves to Olympia, Washington, and accepts a position as attorney general in Licensing Division; teaches French at Evergreen College
1995 Moves to Paris and accepts a position at a French law firm
1997 Becomes the first American to be admitted to the Paris bar
1999 Publishes *Project Girl*, which is named a Best Book of 1999 by the *Los Angeles Times*
2000 National public appearance on "This American Life: Americans in Paris" with Ira Glass
2001 Publishes *Spellbound*, an American Library Association Best Book for Young Adults and International Reading Association Young Adults' Choice
2002 Publishes *Chill Wind*; an American Library Association Quick Pick for Young Adults
2003 Wins the Coretta Scott King/John Steptoe New Talent Award for *Chill Wind*; publishes *Twists and Turns*, which is selected as Booklist Editors' Choice and American Library Association Quick Pick for Young Adults; *Spellbound* translated into French and published as *Brooklyn Babies*
2004 Publishes *Brother Hood*; *Chill Wind* translated into French and published as *Top Rondes*

2005   Diagnosed with cancer; completes rewrite of *Harlem Hustle*

2006   Publishes *Harlem Hustle*; *Twists and Turns* translated into French and published as *Des Tift et du Taf*

2007   Publishes *Off-Color*; passes away at Hôpital Universitaite Paul-Brousse in Villejuif Cedex on April 11; a memorial service held on April 16 at Cimetière du Père-Lachaise; virtual memorial established online on May 1; remains encrypted on May 4 at Greenwood Cemetery in Brooklyn; public memorial service held June 6 at the Schomburg Center for Research and Black Culture in New York City; scholarship fund established at Vassar College in McDonald's honor; *Brother Hood* translated into French and published as *Frères de rap*

Preface

I discovered Janet McDonald in 1999 while browsing the African American section at a local bookstore. I have always been drawn to rough and gritty memoirs that chart the life of one person or another. *Project Girl* was propped on the New Releases shelf, which caught my attention. The blurbs on the back cover made promises of a spectacular read so I had to purchase the book. I found myself transfixed by *Project Girl*. The prose is raw and unnerving while at the same time awe inspiring and honest. Are not memoirs supposed to give their authors a lacquer finish of perfection? Who could be this honest? I finished reading *Project Girl* and found myself wanting more. I immediately made my way to the bookstore for the next installment, but there was none. What followed later from Janet McDonald, however, were six young adult novels.

In the fall of 2001, I taught an English course that featured black female protagonists from varying backgrounds. I included texts that focused on ghetto girls, finishing-school girls, college girls, and yes, project girls. *Project Girl* was included. While several of the texts did not resonate with my mostly white, middle-class university students, *Project Girl* was different. Several of the women in the course wanted more. They saw themselves in the text. The students in my course connected with McDonald's confusion and her self-destructive actions that ironically served to enhance her success. My students all told instances of having "been there." Once the course was over, the project girl's voice would not be silenced in my mind. I knew Janet had more to say. Luckily that fall the first of McDonald's young adult novels, *Spellbound*, was released. I was again impressed by the honesty in her portrayal of the characters and the risks she must have taken to write a young adult novel that included unwed teen mothers.

In 2004, I contacted McDonald regarding this biocritical study. I received an immediate response and so this project began. Over the past few years, I have read all of McDonald's books several times. The story changes with every reading. While her novels are slender, their message is powerful. The characters are lively and outspoken. These adolescent characters all have something in common with McDonald. Either they struggle with finishing high school or they are in the throes of reconciling their dual identities as talented students and streetwise kids. Such a balance is not easily struck.

Over the course of a few years, McDonald and I have corresponded by e-mail, at conferences, and via the public relations staff at Farrar, Straus, Giroux. Although McDonald immediately extended an invitation for a meeting in Paris, France, where she lived, it was not until the spring of 2007 that I was able to visit her. Once in Paris, I traveled from the airport to the center city on the metro. As the train rolled through each suburb, I tried to imagine what life is like for black female adolescents in Paris. I wondered if they read McDonald's work. I wondered how many project girls live in Paris. What did McDonald's family think of her memoir? Do the young adults in her own family read her novels?

Finally, the time had come to visit Janet McDonald to begin a series of interviews. Exiting the metro from the Trocadero station, I braved the cobblestone roads and maniacal traffic so typical of Paris at rush hour. Janet's apartment was located in the Sixteenth Arrondissement, an area known as *the* neighborhood of the wealthy. I was tickled by the fact that a project girl lived here among the rich. Janet always had a knack for getting herself into places where she was not meant to be. Moreover, not only did Janet live in an exclusive neighborhood, her apartment was located above the Musée Clemenceau, the former home and current museum of Georges Clemenceau, a famous author and politician from Paris. The museum was established and opened to the public in 1931 in order to preserve the memory of Clemenceau. Once I entered the courtyard, I imagined Janet sitting at one of the tables nearby jotting down story ideas. At the end of my climb of the five-story walk-up, I was greeted by one of Janet's friends, who gave me a tour of the apartment. Marvelous! The place was sparsely decorated, with a few photos of family members and enough furnishings to make for comfort without clutter. I was intrigued by the desk that sat in the center of the room where Janet writes. Why the center? Why not facing the window? The simplicity of her home is in direct contrast to the complexity of her work. According to Janet, we see what we want to see, but there is always more there. This study, then, confirms her statement.

Although the time spent in Janet's apartment is integral to this study, it is with sadness that I must mention the fact that, at the time of my visit, Janet was in the hospital fighting the battle of all battles—cancer. She stated emphatically that the truth mattered to her, and as a result, she felt it was necessary that I visit her in the hospital. I could not decide whether or not I felt a tinge of guilt and selfishness for meeting with her; however, in the countless interviews she has granted, one theme has prevailed. Janet has a passion for her work, and she wants her readers to understand the meaning in her writing. Such information cannot come through speculation or via e-mail and phone. I wanted Janet to have a voice in this project.

Leaving her apartment enroute to Hôpital Universitaite Paul-Brousse, I examined the questions that I had prepared to ask and decided that I would ask only one—what do you want your readers to take away from your work? I decided that a global question such as this would give Janet the opportunity to say whatever she wanted about her writing and about her life. Yet, I knew that despite the circumstances, I was in for a treat. In fact, earlier that morning, Janet had called my hotel and, speaking in French, pretended to be the front desk ringing in with a wake-up call. Recognizing my puzzlement, she burst into laughter. A sense of humor, even during difficult times, is yet another thread that is woven throughout her work.

Upon my arrival at Paul-Brousse, I tapped on Janet's hospital room door and slowly pushed it open to find her patiently waiting. In our earlier phone conversations, she had warned me of the disarray of her appearance—a headband covered the once-curly hair that had grown straight since the beginning of her treatment. Her perception of disarray was my confirmation that, in fact, self-perception is often more critical than what others see. Janet was beautiful. She looked exactly as she does in her photos. No airbrushing there. Wearing blue pajamas and a matching headband instead of the ubiquitous backless hospital gown, Janet appeared ready for a steady stream of questions.

As the interview progressed, Janet and I were continually interrupted by the doctors and nurses who came in to monitor her care, and by visitors, telephone calls, and Janet's preparation of tea for us both. Once things calmed down in her room, Janet and I lost track of time as we dove into the body of her work. Janet began with a conversation about the current state of her life. She was worried that her disease might end her writing career right at the moment when she had so many stories left to tell.

Janet had numerous friends from all over the world, and many of those acquaintances were made as a result of the publication of her memoir, *Project Girl*. Many of the friendships evolved from casual encounters on airplanes and subways. Janet explained that, although she often wore her Projectgirl.com T-shirt in an effort to promote her book, many people recognized her even when she was not wearing it. While she enjoyed being recognized by so many people, she often felt overwhelmed as well because while writing her memoir was a cathartic experience for her, it was also a cathartic release for some of her readers. Janet often received letters from readers who thanked her for her honesty and candor. These readers also shared their own stories of pain and struggle. She believed the constant flow of letters and e-mails from readers was one of the most rewarding aspects of becoming an author. However, the continual sharing of experiences and feelings weighed heavily on her psyche. Some of the stories invoked in her a sense of relief that she had survived her trauma; other stories frightened her, because it was painful to know that there are so many people whose experienced pain so much greater than she ever had to face.

The notoriety that came with the publication of *Project Girl* forced Janet to become more adept at setting boundaries. In her interview with Thomas Kennedy, she talked a lot about the moment she realized that she had shared too much of her life with the public. Beyond being offered a chance "to explore new opportunities" by her Paris law firm as a result of the publication of her memoir, through her appearances on talk shows such as *Leeza* and *The Rosie O'Donnell Show*, Janet came to terms with the fact that she had exposed herself to the world in a raw and intense manner. Instead of feeling regret about the fallout from the memoir's publication, Janet decided to accept the fact that writing the book was necessary as a release for her and it helped so many readers feel a sense of validation about their own lives.

Coming to terms with the identity that the memoir helped to shape for her, Janet moved on to continue to balance her public self with her private self by staying attached to her readers, but at the same time taking better care of herself in terms of maintaining a certain amount of distance from her public identity. She admits that one of the benefits of writing such a forthright book is that readers feel like they have known her forever, and thus they feel comfortable with asking her to share her own time with them.[1] Presented in the following pages is what I learned from Janet McDonald, *the* original project girl.

Note

1. T. Kennedy, "Up from Brooklyn: An Interview with Janet McDonald," *Literary Review: An International Journal of Contemporary Writing* no. 44 (4) (Summer 2001): 704–20.

~

Acknowledgments

The journey from idea to document has been a long one. I owe many thanks to those who have helped me along the way. I am especially grateful to the late Janet McDonald for her kindness, generosity, and friendship over the past few years; I would like to thank Roberta Seelinger Trites for giving me my start; the English department at the University of North Carolina Wilmington where this project began; Stephanie Hughes and Jeanne McDermott of Farrar, Straus, and Giroux Publishers; the dean's office in the College of Education and Human Services at Cleveland State University that provided the course release and the travel funds in order for me to complete the final stages of this work; Samia Marais of OEIL Public Photography Studio, Paris; Kokie Adams; all of my students, both past and present; my family and a host of friends who gave me words of encouragement; Rupert; and Lauren Stroud for her love, patience, and flexibility. You are the heart of this book.

~

CHAPTER ONE

The Original Project Girl: Humble Beginnings

Janet McDonald was born on August 10, 1953. Her mother went into labor after midnight, during a thunderstorm. Her life has been full of adventure right from the start.[1] On the way to the hospital, the first taxi that the McDonalds hailed broke down on the way, so they were forced to hail another cab in order to arrive at the hospital in time for Janet's birth. According to McDonald, it was necessary for her to learn to be optimistic from the start. Although she laments being born into a world that does not value her identity as a black female from a poor family, McDonald reminds her readers that a sense of humor can make a difference between success and failure. She remarks, "What do you do when your life is set up to be as rough as possible? You just have to focus on the good parts." And there are many good parts about McDonald's life. She balances her narratives by sharing her triumphs along with her struggles in order to inspire hope in her readers.

Although McDonald identifies herself as *the* project girl, Janet's mother, Florence Birdsong, is really the original project girl. Undaunted by southern racism, the McDonalds held onto their belief in the American Dream. Thus, like many southern African American families during the Great Depression, Florence Birdsong and Willie McDonald fled the Jim Crow South and migrated to New York in search of jobs and decent housing. Willie McDonald's arrival in New York and his new job as a postal worker affirmed his faith in the American Dream. It also facilitated his ability to marry Ms. Birdsong and to begin a family.

While McDonald's migration to New York is unremarkable in that countless others followed the same path, it is remarkable that he had very little formal education and therefore was a self-taught man. McDonald recognized his limited opportunities due to his lack of education and thus stressed to his children his belief in academic excellence and its power to transform humble existences into substantial living. For Janet, it was not difficult to make her father's dreams become reality. A self-described "middle of the middle child," Janet excelled in school to a point where she was double-promoted from second grade into the fourth grade. Although all of the McDonald siblings did well in school, Janet outshone everyone else. Her parents were in awe of her abilities, but they were also frightened by her talents.

Mr. McDonald focused on the cultivation of family life within his household. The McDonald family was part of a large population of New Yorkers who lived in government housing during the early 1950s. According to Janet, the projects of her childhood were remarkably different from the projects of today. The McDonald family was considered one of the "founding families" of Farragut Homes in Brooklyn; the homes had been built about the time they arrived in New York, which made it possible for them to be the first tenants in the complex. In fact, Janet's mother remains a Farragut Homes resident today. The community was described as close-knit, quiet, clean, and friendly. There were community centers and neighborhood associations. Parents worked together to keep their children safe. Residents enjoyed the surroundings so much that they spent vast amounts of time sitting outdoors getting to know one another. More important, however, was that one of the main requirements for being able to reside in public housing during the early years was that there could be no single-parent households and that there must be a working adult in the family. The employment requirements for the tenants created a significantly different environment than what we have come to accept as the current project lifestyle.

According to Janet, while the projects were idyllic living spaces and the tenants felt pride for their accomplishments, they hoped for more. They looked forward to the available jobs in the city and hoped that

Janet in 1958, age 4

Janet in 1961, age 8

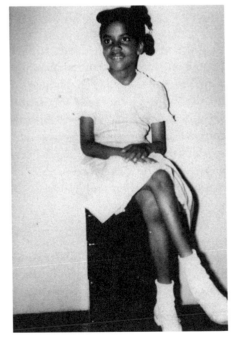

those jobs could provide an opportunity for the families to move out of the projects and into affordable housing. Although some families needed some public assistance to supplement their salaries, they did not view the receiving of public aid as a way of life. Compared to today, when welfare has lost much of its stigma, during the 1950s government assistance was looked down upon. This sense of pride, too, created a hopeful and progressive environment in Farragut Homes. As a working man, Mr. McDonald gave his family a direct connection with the notions of economic mobility and the importance of education.

The McDonald family did everything together. They did chores, ate meals, studied, and, according to Janet, received discipline collectively. The close familial bond extended itself to their outside community, where there were recreational activities and sporting events. The landscape of the community was parklike, clean, and peaceful. There were Keep Off the Grass signs on the green spaces. There were swings and playground areas. The residents sat on benches and watched the children play. There was no violence, and as a whole, there was pride about the community. Given the almost tranquil environment in which the McDonalds lived, then, Janet's early experiences were positive and built self-esteem.

One reason why Janet experienced such a stable childhood was that she thought of her father as Superman. She understood that Superman was a fictional character, but her father's attributes mirrored some of the traits of the heroic figure. It was Janet's father who instilled a positive sense of self in all of his children. Mrs. McDonald was a strong, caring, and intelligent role model who saw her job as caretaker and supporter of her family. She often made decisions about the family independently, but together they saw their marriage as a partnership and thus modeled their ideologies about community and connection for their children.

A Changing Environment

Janet's early childhood home was conducive to the building of a strong sense of community. However, by the 1970s Farragut Homes, like other housing projects across the country, experienced a devastating shift. Coupled with the downturn of sufficient employment opportunities and the growth in single-parent homes, the neighborhood's landscape and mood changed for the worse. Unable to gain decent employment, many young African Americans in Janet's community succumbed to negative means of survival. There had been a time when those who did not graduate from high school could still get a decent job in a factory and were thus able to support themselves and their families. Instead, these same youth were now banished to the streets, where they saw criminal activity, violence, and drug sales and consumption as a viable alternative. Even those who did manage to earn their high school diplomas learned early that the job shortage lowered their chances of finding work. As a result, an atmosphere of hopelessness and discontent replaced the dreamlike moods of the past.

The effects of the expanding underclass and the growing discontent trickled down to even the strongest family units in Farragut Homes—the McDonald family included. Mr. McDonald mourned the days when his community was filled with hope and prosperity. He witnessed a growing number of families deteriorating. He saw once-innocent children transformed into hardened, anger-filled adolescents. He watched the landscape of his neighborhood worsen. Cleanliness and order were replaced with filth and chaos. Most significant, however, Mr. McDonald's dream of his children becoming successful academically and leaving the projects quickly faded. In his own words, Mr. McDonald described the transformation of the population of his community as going from "residents" to "recipients, who will either end up dead or in jail" (*Project Girl* 21).

In his opinion, residents were those Farragut families who made a commitment to the neighborhood by maintaining a peaceful, crime-free environment. These mostly two-parent homes included a working father and a stay-at-home mother who encouraged their children not to see their life in the projects as a stopping point. In fact, many of the Farragut residents came to the neighborhood with the purpose of obtaining a safe place to raise their children until they could save enough money to buy their own homes outside of the projects.

Recipients, according to Mr. McDonald, were the opposite of residents. Welfare recipients did not envision a life outside of the projects nor did they make positive contributions to the overall environment of the neighborhood. Most of these families were single-parent households with a mother who collected welfare from the state. Without a working adult in the home, many of the children in these families had no role models to demonstrate the importance of self-sufficiency. As a result, many of the children in these families did not see full-time work as their legacy. Many of these children grew up to become young adults who often dropped out of high school and thus had nothing constructive to do on a daily basis, which led to their growing participation in criminal activity or drug involvement. The departure of the more stable families from Farragut, then, was the catalyst for the shift from the "resident" mentality among Farragut families to the "recipient" mindset that infected the remaining founding families of the housing project.

A Permanent Underclass

Like others, the McDonalds' motivation for leaving the racist South was that their chances for economic and social mobility were stifled. But the irony of the great migration was that a metropolis once known as the "North" transformed into a different version of the Jim Crow South. Instead of sharecropping for a living, where one was paid a miniscule amount of money for a maximum amount of work, there was unemployment. Instead of segregated schools, there were semi-integrated schools where the teachers focused the majority of their attentions on the white students, while having low expectations of the African American students. Furthermore, instead of Jim Crow signs forbidding blacks to enter stores, theaters, and restaurants, there were segregated neighborhoods where families could acquire their basic necessities, but travel from the immediate community was rare. Most ironic, however, as whites quickly relocated to get away from blacks, the "resident" sector of blacks in Farragut Homes moved away in order to distance themselves from fellow blacks who were a part of the destructive "recipient" population.

The spirit of the McDonald household changed as well. Coupled with the tensions between her home environment and her school environment, Janet's grades began to fall. While the McDonald parents struggled with Janet's slump in her educational success, they also battled the evils of their environment. Somehow, despite all of the coaching and encouragement that was doled out to the children, despite Mr. McDonald's constant refrain of "Be careful or you will end up dead or in jail," some of his children made bad choices. Several of them, Janet included, used drugs. Luke, the eldest son, came out as a homosexual; his father sent him to Alabama rather than accept his son's identity. It seemed as though the McDonald family was falling apart.

Out of the Projects and into Books

High school was difficult for Janet. At the end of junior high school, Janet applied for and was accepted by a gifted program at Erasmus Hall Academy in the Flatbush section of Brooklyn. Admission to this school meant that Janet's trip to classes took nearly an hour by train and bus. While she was identified as academically gifted, she earned marginal grades in her coursework. She says that her academic performance had much to do with not only her lack of applying herself, but also with feelings of being slighted by the teachers at Erasmus. She explains, "The white teachers [at Erasmus] seemed primarily concerned with the progress of the white students. I was stung by their lack of interest in me and started skipping classes" (*Project Girl* 27). Coupled with Janet's sense that the teachers at Erasmus were not invested in the black students' education were Janet's feelings of inadequacy in terms of her own intellectual abilities. Where she once excelled as a top student in her old school, where she competed with students who received the same caliber of education and lived the same lifestyle as she, Erasmus introduced her to another world of experience. The students at Erasmus came from a different level of educational expectations. Since Erasmus Academy was an elite school, her peers included children of the wealthy and well traveled. Moreover, these students were groomed to be leaders and thus took for granted the excellence in educational opportunities that their race and class afforded them. Academic competition at Erasmus precipitated feelings of insecurity for Janet, so much so that she rarely spoke up in class; outside of class, she sat in on political discussions but contributed nothing. At home, she began to expand her music and reading tastes to include classical music and literary classics. Janet made it her business to catch up as best she could to her peers in an academic sense.

Socially, catching up was more difficult. Most of the students existed in a social sphere beyond what she could imagine. Moreover, not only was Janet forced to cope with the social exclusion doled out to her by the white middle-class and upper-class students, she also had to adjust to the exclusion from her fellow black students as well. More often than not, the social isolation had more to do with the issue of class than of race. For instance, a black classmate named Judy had no interest in becoming friends with Janet. No matter what strategy Janet employed to get Judy's attention, she failed. Another black student, Indigo, a politically and academically adept male student at Erasmus, amazed Janet with his knowledge; however, a friendship did not develop.

Janet's attendance at Erasmus exacerbated her feelings of not belonging. The trip across town to Erasmus was a universe away from her at-home reality. At school, the teachers mustered up little sympathy for her long trip to school that sometimes resulted in her arriving late to class. The teachers did not seem to care about her academic progress in the same way they invested in their white students' futures, and although her classmates were adept at spouting political beliefs about social justice and political equality, their vision of the "other" was not expanded enough for them to realize that every student at Erasmus was not just like them. At home, Janet struggled with rapid neighborhood decline that left her confused about her own future. Since some of Janet's siblings had entered the downward spiral of violence and drugs, Mrs. McDonald kept a watchful eye on her remaining children for fear that they would be next to fall. Unfortunately, however, Janet's parents did not recognize the agony and confusion she felt as an alien in each of her environments of school and home. Janet explains:

I was straddling contradictory worlds and not fitting in anywhere. Not in my own family, where I was white-girl-in-residence, not in the new projects, and not at Erasmus, where I was tolerated mostly for the sheer pathos of my "please be my friend" presentation. (*Project Girl*, 30)

Despite her struggles, McDonald graduated from Erasmus Hall Academy with only a general studies diploma. That, coupled with the realization that she and her family had been unaware that the college application deadlines had passed, made her begin to feel as if she had no future. At the same time, Mrs. McDonald began to lose hope that

Janet as a teenager

at least one of her children would be spared from the violence and drugs in their neighborhood. Mrs. McDonald was so worried that she often pressured Janet to take a job working at the telephone company so that she could at least have steady employment, but Janet refused. She had other plans. Although she had finished high school, Janet had not earned the academic diploma needed to qualify for college.

She attended summer school and night school until she earned her academic credentials.

While Mr. McDonald held on to hopes that at least one of his children would fulfill his dream, his hope began to waiver. He was tentative when Janet informed him about her plans to enroll in the Harlem Preparatory Program—a program that would eventually land her a scholarship and admission into a reputable college. Mrs. McDonald, too, had begun to lose hope. When not pressuring Janet to seek employment, Mrs. McDonald chided her daughter about her incessant reading and her lack of what she termed "common sense." At one point, Mrs. McDonald ordered Janet to dispose of the books that were cluttering up the house.

Due to her success in the Harlem Prep Program, Janet won scholarship money for college. As part of that program, admission interviews and campus visits were arranged for her. Janet's first college selection, she explains, was based on the name of the college—Briarcliff College. Her visit to the campus, however, made her aware of her bad choice. According to Janet, Briarcliff College "was a finishing school for debutantes who rode horses" (*Project Girl* 49). At the advice of one of the counselors at Harlem Prep, Janet applied and was admitted to Vassar College.

Identity Crisis

Janet's journey from Harlem Prep to Vassar was not smooth. Like many participants in programs such as Harlem Prep and A Better Chance (ABC) that were available to minority students labeled as gifted, Janet struggled with issues of identity that centered around her ambivalence regarding her gender, race, and class. Harlem Prep was a supportive program in that the curriculum prepared its participants academically and sometimes emotionally. In fact, following Janet's visit to Briarcliff College, the administrators of Harlem Prep allowed her to remain in the program an additional year so that she could adjust to the idea of leaving home to attend college in an environment that would be alien to her. Although supportive in many important ways, however, the Harlem Prep Program did not prepare their students to confront and move past issues regarding class and race. Much of Janet's ambivalence regarding attending Briarcliff had to do with her not being ready to leave her community. Having endured most of her childhood with a sense that she did not fit in anywhere, the Harlem Prep program gave her that sense of community she longed for.

Moreover, several events that took place while she was a student at Prep gave her insight into the harsh realities of growing up. While at Harlem Prep, Janet balanced her growing ability to bond and make solid friendships with students from the same background as she. The difference, however, was that these friendships were developed in the context of working toward success. The connection with these students gave her encouragement as they were all working toward the same goal. Gaining friends and then witnessing the decline of fellow students who got caught up in drugs and other tragedies acted as a reminder to Janet that adolescence can be fragile. Just as there is a possibility to change one's life, the evils of the past can come back to destroy progress. Carlton, a fellow prep student, succumbed to a drug overdose that ended his life. Janet's reaction spoke volumes to her about how easy it is to overlook the blessing of camaraderie and respect in a quest to self-destruct. With a history of feeling isolated, the warm cocoon of Harlem Prep was what Janet needed all along.

In the fall of 1971, the McDonald family arrived at the Vassar College campus in the family's station wagon filled with mismatched suitcases. Janet's father had long spoken of education as "the ticket" out of the projects. Janet's arrival at Vassar was the beginning of his growing pride and hope that one of his children would make good on his wishes. Having requested a single room, but assigned a double room instead, Janet encountered one of her first struggles as a co-ed on a predominantly white campus populated by mostly wealthy students. The Erasmus Hall Academy experience seemed to be repeating itself. Janet's roommate, Brenda, was an African American Californian from a wealthy family. Brenda sparked in Janet an anxiety regarding race and class that set the tone for her first semester at Vassar. Janet's family was not familiar with any wealthy black people; they did not know of such a possibility. As Janet and Brenda began to settle into their routine as roommates, Janet spent time comparing herself to Brenda. Brenda arrived with multiple suitcases and several more were in the process of being shipped. Janet's belongings filled only two drawers and very little closet space in their dorm room. There was a different aura about Brenda. She seemed to be happy all of the time to the point where her cheeriness annoyed Janet. Brenda's presence awakened Janet's latent resentment about being born into a poor family. Not only was Janet concerned about not being able to measure up to her white peers socially and financially, but Vassar's campus added an additional burden—connecting with black people who were unlike herself.

Throughout Janet's childhood, her siblings teased her for being lighter skinned than the rest of the family and for being bookish, and "college material." Janet felt conflicted about these labels given her by her siblings because, as she saw it, her skin tone and her academic prowess afforded her no more privilege than any other black child growing up in Brooklyn. The level of tension between the McDonald siblings grew when Janet enrolled at Erasmus. Her older sister Ann began telling Janet that her attendance at that school would turn her into a "straight-back Sally," or a white girl. At Erasmus, Janet's lack of self-awareness caused her to seek acceptance from her peers by stealing records from a music store and passing them out to her classmates. Her uncertainty also caused her to be a discipline problem in class as she found herself joining in with her peers who rebelled against school rules and skipped classes. Janet's struggle with her racial identity lay dormant until her arrival at Vassar. She was haunted by fears of turning into a straight-back Sally. She and her family worried that attending Vassar would move her further away from an emotional connection with her black self and her black community.

Janet's feelings of a split self, her double consciousness, was a catalyst for her cycle of acting out during her first semester at Vassar. In order to fight her fear of an impending transformation into a white girl, Janet tried to hold on tight to her project girl identity by speaking with an affected tone of confrontation and by constantly reminding those who would listen that she was a tough girl from the projects.

As the semester progressed, she concluded that in order to be a real project girl, she must act like one. To Janet, one of the project girl markers was heroin use. Janet's adventurous nature and her naïve sense of invincibility led her to travel from the suburban community of Vassar to the streets of Harlem, where she purchased drugs. Her behavior was so risky that she aimlessly went to various drug houses in Harlem in order to find the necessary paraphernalia for injecting the substance. Back on campus, the same feelings that led her to steal records for her peers in high school returned, as she felt the need to not only take the drugs, but also to let everyone know that she was doing so. She shared heroin with several of her friends and sometimes after ingesting a dose, she made a public spectacle of herself by performing antics that she, at the time, thought made her look cool. Once word on campus spread that she had drug connections, Janet was tasked with traveling back and forth to Harlem to buy drugs for her campus friends. Such assignments fooled her into believing that her actions were connected to her project roots.

In an interview, McDonald remarked that she now understands that her feelings were a form of survivor's guilt. Before her departure to college, Janet's siblings struggled with school and the social decline of their neighborhood. Janet was made aware of this downward spiral of her neighborhood via letters and calls from home. Each time Janet spoke to or received a letter from home, the contents included descriptions of friends and neighbors who were killed, arrested, or drug addicted. Janet compared her situation to theirs and felt guilty that she was not there to help her community. Worse than these feelings of inadequacy was her guilt at being spared the torture of watching firsthand what was going on in her community and her social isolation due to her reputation as "one with a problem." She attempted suicide. Her attempt, however, was unsuccessful because the college infirmary had prescribed placebos instead of the sleeping pills that she had requested. Janet admits to being thankful that the doctors on Vassar's campus had been able to foresee the results of prescribing sleeping pills to particular students. The next day, Janet recounted the suicide attempt to her therapist, for which she was confined to the campus infirmary for fear that she was a danger to herself. As a result of an attempted escape, she was released from Vassar College on medical leave in order to get help for her problems. The following morning Janet was in the family station wagon and on her way back to Farragut Homes.

The Return of Icarus

Back in Brooklyn, Janet immediately realized that Farragut Homes was no longer a place for her. She saw firsthand all of the gory tales that had been relayed to her via mail and telephone. She confronted the fact that she had become, though only by small measure, a different person. In a matter of a few months, she had been taken out of the projects and resocialized into someone with the advantage of opportunity and access. She recognized, too, that she did indeed want to exist in a world that would allow her to maintain her black, project girl identity, but that would also allow her to partake in the advantages that education and wealth would grant her. In short, Janet's return home was what precipitated her drive to get away from home. In order to prepare herself for a return to college, Janet busied herself with therapy sessions, writing letters to friends and former professors, and cultivating a relationship with her younger brother Kevin, while at the same time, she longed to get as far away from Farragut as possible.

Janet's discomfort with home and the realization that she wanted to experience more opportunity was the driving force in her decision to run away. She decided that her destination would be California. Armed with a few belongings and forty-five dollars that she had saved, she arranged a ride from an advertisement in the *Village Voice*, but she only made it as far as Wysox, Pennsylvania, where she became a member of a commune. Janet's time away from home and school gave her perspective. At Wysox, she was accepted by the members of the commune because they believed that she had been sent to them by an act of their god, Guru Maharaj Ji, the fourteen-year-old master of the commune's religious group, the premies. She described the summer she spent at the commune as the happiest period in her life because she was baptized as a premie before leaving the farm and returning to Vassar. Janet's time at the commune mentally prepared her for a second chance at college, and in the following fall, she returned to Vassar. Janet was officially out of the projects and back into books.

Janet's fall 1973 return to Vassar was successful. She earned good grades and found an area of study that excited her—French literature. Although her French-speaking skills were weak and despite the reaction from friends and family because of her chosen major, Janet went forward with her plans to participate in a junior year, study-abroad program in Paris. Not only did Janet find her niche in terms of fitting in academically at Vassar, she also began to complicate her understanding of the dimensions of race and class. She explained, "The reality of social diversity supplanted her clichéd world of 'rich white girls' and 'boogie blacks'" (*Project Girl* 85). Similarly, Janet's self-imposed social isolation lessened as she came to realize that she was not alone in the quest to find comfort in environments and cultures that were different from her own. Janet realized that "she was no more an outsider than an Indian feminist or a Puerto Rican Southerner or a Harlem teenager who kept horses at her family's upstate ranch" (*Project Girl* 85). Armed with her newfound faith in the Guru Maharaj and her resolve to get her college degree, Janet took advantage of the opportunity to expand her social outlook by befriending new and different kinds of people and traveling whenever she got the chance.

Janet's study-abroad experience broadened her understanding of the complexities of American racial and social categories. While in Paris, Janet recognized that American society treated race differently than did the French. She explained that not having to reconcile the project girl–Vassar girl duality on a daily basis gave her the opportunity to experience the freedom that comes with being defined by one's nationality instead of one's race. For instance, Janet realized that she was not viewed as a black person; she was seen as an American. Thus the stereotypes and myths attached to American identity applied to her, not the stereotypes and myths of blackness. The viewing of Americans as a collective, while still problematic, was not nearly as confining as American racial categorization. In the United States, Janet understood that all of her actions, negative and positive, were viewed as characteristic of blacks. Janet described this experience as being "free of the burden of race, while still experiencing blackness."[2] She wrote, "I no longer had to worry about making African Americans look good. Or bad. Whatever I did was attributed to Americanness, not blackness" (*Project Girl* 91). Being able to focus on herself from a different standpoint, then, helped Janet take the focus off her own life and problems in order to be able to develop an appreciation for French culture.

By the time graduation arrived, Janet had transformed herself from the project girl who wrestled with life outside of familiar surroundings to a young adult who craved the freedom of anonymity that she experienced in Paris. The fall after her graduation, Janet went back to Paris to study French literature at the Sorbonne. The study abroad trip two years earlier changed her life because it provided for her an

Farragut Homes,
Janet's childhood home

Janet's home in Paris

environment that she craved. She shared that the freedom from worry about whether or not she styled her hair or ironed her clothes before leaving her apartment was a freedom that she had searched for all along. She felt liberated from the strict racial categories that preceded all of the other aspects of her identity: intelligence, personality, and self-worth. Janet explained that while racism in France is far from nonexistent, it is circumscribed in a manner that benefits American minorities. Black people from Africa are disdained by the French because they are seen as those who come to Paris not to contribute to the culture and economy, but instead, to reap the benefits of it. Janet calls this difference the "French paradox."[3] She explains that the French paradox is a combination of racial prejudice toward blacks from African countries, with the nonidentification of racial prejudice for African Americans. Janet wondered how it is that "the French can love me but hate someone who looks just like me?"[4]

In an effort to figure out the mystery of the French paradox, Janet concluded that much of the discrimination that nonwhite people in France experience has to do with social and economic class.[5] To begin with, the perception that most Americans come to France as tourists leads many French people to assume that Americans are well off. However, a significant number of black Africans immigrate to France. Their immigrant status often locks them in a cycle of poverty, which means that they rely on France's social programs. These housing developments are similar to American housing projects, where there is a high concentration of poverty and joblessness, which inevitably fuels crime activity, drug trafficking, and violence. However, American housing projects are mainly located within central cities; albeit separated by highways or railroad tracks they are at least in close proximity to many public resources.[6] Housing projects or *banlieues* in Paris are located in the suburbs away from all of the jobs, hospitals, and grocery stores.[7] Since many of the African immigrants do not own cars, they have to rely on Paris's metro system. Unfortunately, most of the buses and metro lines do not have routes to these suburban areas.

For example, Clichy-Sous-Bois residents suffer economically and socially because of the commune's isolated location, which results in a high unemployment rate and social unrest.[8] Clichy-Sous-Bois is located nine miles outside of Paris, but there is not sufficient transportation to the suburb.[9] There are no rail stations or Paris metro stations in Clichy;

the closest rail station is two miles away in the neighboring commune called Le Raincy. There is only one bus in and out of Clichy; however, that bus does not travel into any metropolitan areas of Paris. Furthermore, having a suburban address or an African or Muslim-sounding name precludes many Clichy residents from obtaining work because employers look at the name and address and if it hints of immigrant status, the application is thrown away. The practice of job discrimination leaves the majority of African immigrants unemployed and further isolated from the central city's resources. The residents of the French suburbs such as Clichy, then, experience a double-edged sword because they are stuck in a pattern of unemployment and social isolation that fuels the stereotypes about them.

Based on her knowledge of the obstacles faced by non-American blacks in Paris, Janet, then, came to understand, though not appreciate, the discrimination aimed at Africans. Coming of age in a Brooklyn housing project and being treated the same as the youth in Clichy kept her grounded in the knowledge that although she experienced a particular brand of racial freedom, she must never forget that she *is* a project girl.

Notes

1. Author profile, Farrar, Straus, Giroux Books for Young Readers Biographical Information Website, www.fsgkidsbooks.com/authordetails.asp?ID= McDonald (accessed January 30, 2007).

2. Janet McDonald, interview by Ira Glass, *This American Life*, Chicago Public Radio, Paris, France, August 24, 2001.

3. *This American Life*, August 24, 2001.

4. *This American Life*, August 24, 2001.

5. "A Sister in Paris: American African Woman in Paris, France." *Essence Magazine* 25, no. 1 (May 1, 1994): 54.

6. Sudhir Venkatesh, *American Project* (Cambridge, MA: Harvard University Press, 2000).

7. Ann-Louise Shapiro, *Housing the Poor of Paris* (Madison: University of Wisconsin Press, 1985).

8. The October 2005 riots in Clichy-Sous-Bois are one example.

9. Craig Smith, "Inside French Housing Project, Feelings of Being the Outsiders," *New York Times*, November 9, 2005, p. 1A.

CHAPTER TWO

~

On Becoming a Writer:
Project Girl

At the age of forty-six, when she wrote *Project Girl*, Janet McDonald did not fit the prototypical model of the memoir author. To begin with, she was not famous nor was she elderly. She grew up poor and in the projects. More important, McDonald was black and female. However, by this time she had returned to Paris to live on a permanent basis and was working as an attorney at a French law firm. A self-identified writer since the age of nine, McDonald's talents evolved from poetry to journal to memoir, on to fiction for adolescents.

She explained that as a child, her writing consisted of "little things like bizarre lists of 'what to buy when grown' (pizza was on it); 'what to wear when grown' (black Hush Puppy shoes and a black dickey); then stories about living alone on an island, about girl renegades."[1] At the age of twelve, McDonald wrote her first book—a dozen stapled pages titled *Build a House on an Island*. McDonald reveals that she moved on to "exceedingly horrible poetry" in high school. She began her official journal in 1979 when she was in her mid-twenties, and she has been journaling ever since.

McDonald continued to write in her journals while she published articles in legal journals. Then, at the encouragement of her friends, she began work on her memoir. McDonald worked as a lawyer by day and wrote her book at night and on weekends and during vacations.

She explains that "writing in my journals was not serious; the writing I published was casual, just for fun. None of it changed my life, but I delighted in it."[2] It was not until a friend suggested that she publish the material in her journals in the form of a memoir that McDonald considered making her private life public, but she remained apprehensive about sharing her writing with her co-workers in Paris. Instead, she began to publicly live what she calls a "double life." According to McDonald, the experience of writing *Project Girl* produced a "recklessly honest and luxuriously cathartic account of coming of age in a New York City housing project. Replete with nervous breakdowns, run-ins with the law and moments when she didn't inhale."[3]

Following the publication of *Project Girl*, McDonald made guest appearances on radio shows, daytime talk shows, and at book signings. At the same time her popularity was growing in the United States, McDonald struggled to keep her celebrity status a secret in Paris. Because she was so candid about her past in *Project Girl*, McDonald felt trepidation about sharing her troubled past with those whose respect she needed in order to be taken seriously as a corporate lawyer in a prestigious law firm. Unfortunately, however, McDonald's secret was revealed. Word of her esteem in the United States traveled to Paris, where the leaders of her law firm became concerned about the connections between *Project Girl* and the reputation of the law firm. At one point, McDonald was admonished by a senior member of her firm for not revealing the publication of her book. Unfortunately, despite the respect that she had garnered in the United States and from various co-workers and friends, the higher-ups in her law firm remained uneasy. Within months of the conversation with the senior member, McDonald was offered a leave of absence to "pursue other interests."

A Full-time Writer at Last

The invitation to pursue other interests released McDonald from the pressures of working as a lawyer by day and writing books during evenings, weekends, and vacations. Her dismissal from the law firm was accompanied by a substantial severance package that could be used for living expenses while she pursued writing as a full-time occupation. It seems, then, that McDonald was liberated from the stresses that come with living a double life. From childhood into adulthood, she felt as if she needed to keep her life a secret. McDonald realized that keeping secrets takes a substantial amount of work. Through the forthright narrative of her memoir, she recognized that she was, in essence, free of her own life's secrets—the good secrets as well as the bad ones.

Janet's freedom to reveal her double identity came at a cost. The publication of *Project Girl* brought with it the vulnerability that comes with self-exposure. She once explained that the feelings expressed in *Project Girl* are raw and angry and, at the same time, innocent. She went on to say, "I cannot believe how naïve I was to appear on worldwide television shows such as *The Leeza Gibbons Show* and *The Rosie O'Donnell Show* to tell the world my business."⁴ McDonald also described particular incidents where her readers felt a kinship with her, so much so that she received letters and calls from people who all thanked her for the honesty within her work. Her readers felt so close to her that she had to quickly learn to set boundaries for herself and her family.

While her first book is a nonfiction tale of growing up in a challenging environment, Janet's fictional work shares similarities with some of the stories in her memoir. All of her work addresses the challenges of growing up in an urban setting (New York) where the characters in the novels have to struggle on a daily basis to hold on to hope and their determination to make the right decisions. Her first work of fiction, *Spellbound*, introduces us to a fictional, albeit plausible, project girl, Raven Jefferson, a high school dropout and teenage parent who dreams of becoming successful and getting her family out of the projects. Like McDonald, Raven receives admission to a college preparatory program that includes a four-year scholarship. Aisha Ingram is the protagonist of the second novel in the series—*Chill Wind*. At the age of nineteen, Aisha learns that she can no longer remain unemployed and on welfare. She gets an opportunity to become a plus-size model—a move which helps to transform her from an unmotivated and hopeless teen to a working professional. The series closes with the final installment of the Project Girl trilogy, *Twists and Turns*, and our introduction to Keeba and Teesha Washington. These twin sisters and fellow project girls are blessed with a mentor who is committed to helping the girls capitalize on their talents as hairstylists and open their own beauty shop.

In her fifth book, McDonald shifts gears as she creates a male protagonist—Nate—who is trapped between two worlds. As an academically talented student, Nate is admitted to a prestigious boarding school in upstate New York. This Harlem-born teen faces the realities of the struggle to remain, no matter what, true to himself. Janet's experiences are similar to Nate's, in that her academic talents landed her first at Erasmus Hall Academy and then into the Harlem Preparatory Program and Vassar College. Janet explained that she wanted Nate to have a different experience than she did as a student at Vassar. While her education was interrupted by emotional turmoil that led to a medical leave, Nate avoids the pitfalls that come with facing an identity crisis. Instead, he prevails as the well-adjusted, academically gifted student who does not fall victim to the social difficulties that come with transplanting oneself to an alien environment. *Harlem Hustle*, Janet's sixth book, is the tale of Eric Samson. Orphaned at an early age, Eric, or "Hustle," as he is known to his friends, has had to make his own way. *Harlem Hustle* gives readers a glimpse into the struggles that urban youth face when their lives start out in deficit mode. Eric, by the novel's end, prevails in his quest to shift from his identity as a petty thief to an entertainer. Along the way, Hustle learns about the importance of family and community as well as the importance of self-respect and perseverance. McDonald explains that her editor found the first draft of the novel inaccessible for too many audiences because of the number of popular and hip-hop culture references that might not be familiar to some readers. Janet's seventh and last novel, *Off-Color*, is a variation of the racial-passing theme found in early American literature and has a surprising twist that ends full circle. *Off-Color*, explained McDonald, was written in its entirety while she was ill.

In each novel, readers get a solid education regarding popular culture, history, current events, literature, and more. What makes McDonald a significant figure in the genre of adolescent literature is that all of her stories are tales of resilience. While a growing number of writers produce realistic prose for contemporary adolescent readers, some of them have not lived the experiences they write about. While there are now more multicultural books that represent the variations of coming-of-age experiences, the majority of literature for adolescent readers still features white, middle-class, and often male protagonists.

As a result, many of the problems that urban teenagers face are not addressed in the literature they read. Texts such as McDonald's are not considered mainstream because of their sociological nature. However, Janet's work has garnered a huge following of readers who can relate to the characters in the novels and who understand the conflict of struggle and hope.

In return for the encouragement that she received from her readers, Janet made it her mission to not only give them humorous stories with plausible characters; she also wanted her readers to learn about the world around them. For instance, in *Spellbound*, Janet mentions the 9/11 attacks in a scene where the novel's protagonist, Raven Jefferson, walks across the Brooklyn Bridge and notices that the landscape is remarkably different now that the Twin Towers are gone. In *Brother Hood*, Nate reads Dostoevsky while riding the commuter train into Grand Central Station. In *Harlem Hustle*, readers are made aware that the former Seneca Village, a settlement for freed black slaves, was overtaken by the government's eminent domain policy in 1857 in order to create what is now known as Central Park. Janet explained that her infusion of history, current events, and literary classics is intentional. "Many of my readers have not heard of these writers and events and exposure to these items only serves to enhance the reading experience of teens." Moreover, McDonald explained, "We have to be mindful of the importance of the literary classics. These texts have stood the test of time and can aid as locations of insight into how we understand our world. Multicultural educators should be ever-mindful of the dangers of supplanting one type of text for another. Instead, a solid integration of knowledge should be put forth to students."[5]

You Can Take the Girl Out of the Projects, But You Can't Take the Projects Out of the Girl

In a 2001 *Village Voice* article titled "Project Girls," Janet McDonald interviews several women, including her own mother, Florence McDonald, regarding project life. McDonald jokingly tells the story of how her mother always chided her with the saying, "You can take the girl out of the projects, but you can't take the projects out of the girl." If we take into consideration the events in *Project Girl*, perhaps the saying rings true. Most of Janet's troubles came about when Farragut Homes was not her primary residence. Early events such as getting caught stealing and skipping school were minor in their effect on Janet's life. However, McDonald's resentment, drug use, attempted suicide, and nervous breakdowns happened at Vassar, the upstate New York environment that was meant as a location for her to thrive. At Cornell University she suffered a violent attack; ironically the stereotype of project life should have meant that such a thing would take place in her home community and not at an elite institution in an upstate suburb. Witnessing such violence had an intense impact upon McDonald's psyche. She suffered sympathy pains for her fellow neighbors: intense guilt, resentment, and anger.

Similarly, Janet's attempts at forming a bicultural identity can be said to be a contributing factor to the pain she faced throughout her adolescence. The culture of a school located outside of the home community has the potential to spark feelings of being caught between two worlds: the home world and the school world. Since students spend most of their waking hours in school settings, the influence of the institution has a tremendous impact on their feelings of affirmation and worth. If the school culture is in direct opposition to the home culture, the adolescent identity will be confronted with countless instances of personal invalidation because the school does not affirm nonwhite traditions of language and culture. In order to compensate for the imbalance in identity affirmation, many adolescents take on a second cultural identification as a strategy to gain and then maintain membership in school settings. Other students in the same predicament reject the idea of taking on another cultural identity in order to survive school. Instead, these students experience school on the fringes and thus tend to perform marginally in terms of integrating school and home cultures, or they give up altogether and perhaps drop out of school. Janet expressed dismay all along regarding her feelings of marginalization in school settings; however, her strategy of reeducating and resocializing herself at Erasmus enabled her to stay afloat and graduate from high school.

Just as school was in direct opposition to home, home culture collided with school culture during nonschool hours. While Janet's parents were supportive of her academic commitment, their actions did not always communicate their feelings. There were countless times when Janet was reminded of her "lack of common sense" by Mrs. McDonald. Janet's siblings often teased her and ultimately labeled her the "resident white girl" because of her academic and social interests. Within the neighborhood of Farragut, none of the neighborhood children traveled with her to Erasmus. Instead, their interests remained concerned with the immediate surroundings of the projects. As a result, the possibility of Janet being able to incorporate her school identity into her home identity was nonexistent, and because she spent so many hours in school, it was difficult for her to let go of the school identity when she was home.

Bicultural identification is often examined from the perspective of outside institutions such as school and work in opposition or companion to home and family. There is a sense that the need to help students cope with social institutions such as school outweighs the need to aid children in learning to integrate social institutions into their home environments. As a result, students often struggle with the forming of a positive sense of identity within themselves because of the tendency to believe that identities formed outside of home are just that—outside. Behaving like a schoolgirl on the playground or at the dinner table is seen as alien behavior.

Linguist Geneva Smitherman explains the phenomenon of code switching in language. Speakers code switch when they transition from one environment to another in order to meet the requirements of a given discourse community where they are present. In this sense, the same can be true for identity performance as well, in that, in order to be accepted as a full member of a given community, one must meet the social protocols of that given setting. Thus, in order for Janet to gain validation in school, she would need to code switch.[6]

To that end, bicultural identification leaves adolescents feeling caught between two worlds due to the fact that this positioning is not integrative, but rather polemic. Moreover, the use of such a strategy is not of much help to adolescents such as Janet, who did, in fact, want all of the dimensions of her identity to be validated without having to hide segments of herself in the process. Thus, leaving Farragut for Flatbush or Vassar was a Herculean task for Janet due to the fact that she did not experience full acceptance from any of the communities in which she came of age. Still, Janet's strong sense of herself as a project girl and as an academician, though separate identities in her own mind, are the aspects of her life that brought her success and thus opened up new possibilities for her. Had she not been a student in the Farragut neighborhood, then she would not have been recognized as gifted. Had she not possessed a strong sense of obligation to being a project girl, then she would not have had a place to return to when she needed respite.

Janet's quest to give up no part of her identity, but instead to add to it, is what makes *Project Girl* a fascinating text. Her refusal to leave her roots behind, too, was the cause of much pain in that she failed to negotiate how much of the past really belonged to her. Why, for instance, did she get involved with drugs at Vassar as a way to hold on to her project identity, when, in fact, she had no drug associations when she lived in Farragut? Similarly, Janet spent her entire childhood in Farragut Homes, but why did she have the looming fear that she would lose her identity and forget her past if she relocated to another part of the country? This desire to hold on to the past was embedded in a quest to control her surroundings in a way that allowed her to at least retain familiarity when everything around her was changing rapidly. With the threat of becoming a white girl, Janet felt the desire to maintain her blackness and her project roots as a way to hold on to herself. Janet was afraid that becoming someone else meant that she would end up leaving the projects for good. In this sense, Janet was and remained committed to the community of Farragut because, despite the fact that she felt alien to the environment in which she grew up, the projects were *in* her.

Storytelling

Project Girl is most often praised for its quality of writing and its significance in terms of getting a perspective on what it means to grow up in the projects; however, Susan Tekluve, for instance, in her review of *Project Girl*, writes that, "Shortly after the jail scene, the book loses its composure, dissolving into a series of journal entries."[7] Tekluve's remarks are consistent with other readers of the text. While section 1 is well written and contains a wonderful story, section 2 is not as fluid, because, according to McDonald, "The writing in part two of the memoir is meant to be fragmented and scattered, because the narrative style gives voice to the fragmented, scattered state of mind that I was in during the time that the events in this section of the book takes place."[8] With McDonald's statement in mind, then, it is important to examine the narrative structure in section 2 of the book.

McDonald opens section 2 with a narrative about her adventures in Paris, where she was enrolled in graduate school; she also agonizes over the eventual death of her father. Section 2 begins solemnly as readers come to understand the ambivalence that McDonald felt at twenty-five. She was a college graduate with a liberal arts degree and no job. She felt compelled to attend law school for two reasons: because she needed a marketable degree and because law school was a dream her parents had for her. While McDonald's feelings of uncertainty are not uncommon for young adults her age, her anxiety was compounded by her father's death. Luckily, Mr. McDonald was able to attend Janet's graduation from Vassar. Since none of Janet's siblings had achieved "the ticket," as Mr. McDonald labeled a college degree, she was his last hope of seeing at least one of his children succeed in school. In *Project Girl*, Janet reflects on her relationship with her father; she describes her resentment and, at the same time, her appreciation for the pressure that her father placed on his children to become successful. Mr. McDonald's dream for all of his children to receive "the ticket," or the belief that education equals freedom, is not uncommon in many homes, and black homes in particular. McDonald mourned her father's death as the end to the one stable thing that held the McDonald family together.

Having been accepted into Cornell Law School, McDonald decided it was time to fulfill her parents' wish. At the age of twenty-six, she enrolled at Cornell, where her academic performance was adequate, but far from stellar. At the advice of one of her law school peers, Janet returned for her second year of law school a few weeks early so that she could compete for a spot on the school's law review. She was raped during the first week she arrived on campus. Like her career at Vassar, Janet's quest for a law degree was interrupted by tragedy. The rape left Janet in so much emotional turmoil that she suffered what her therapists labeled "neurotic episodes."[9] Janet stopped attending classes and was admitted to the psychiatric ward, which meant that her tenure at Cornell turned out to be short lived.

Based on these events, then, it is no wonder that the narration in section 2 of *Project Girl* is a sharp contrast to section 1. Although critics comment on the inconsistency of voice, Janet's use of narration through journal entries is a discursive strategy that is often used in memoirs, especially when the telling of events evokes pain for the writer. Janet explains that she felt like the writing process of the second half of the text was more of an out-of-body experience than the linear and concrete narration in the first half. She says, "I don't remember writing that section of the book and it is probably due to the fact that those days were the darkest in my life. I relied on the journals to give voice to my experiences because the pain is so great that I could not spend time reflecting and then telling those stories."[10]

Burned in Memory

Third-person narration combined with first-person narration deliberately confuses who speaks with who sees, as is the case in McDonald's story. Readers understand that the cause of her mental and physical decline has much to do with the tragedies of her father's death and the subsequent rape. The protagonist-narrator point of view reveals that while Janet's struggles are acknowledged by those around her, she did not get intensive support for learning to deal with the trauma she suffered; instead, she felt angry at herself for not being more careful, and she felt too ashamed to tell her mother what had happened to her. When she finally revealed the incident to her mother, "She sighed and never mentioned it again."[11] Janet's emotional state was so dismal that her therapist canceled her services. Thus, Janet's chaotic state of mind, as it is reflected in the journal entries, is consistent with the chaos of the narrative structure of the text in general. Perry Nodelman explains that journal entries, although structurally different, serve a purpose and thus require readers to use a particular set of reading strategies:

> A journal entry, on the one hand, uses an involved first-person narrator, and an internal character-focalizer, and, because it is assumed to be written for the private purposes of the protagonist-narrator, it is more interested in recording the chronological order of a story than in arranging a plot to create suspense for readers. The meaning of the events

is often far from clear to the narrator, and so such entries are likely to return repeatedly to images and ideas the writer is exploring rather than stating themes.[12]

Janet's multiple mental states are conveyed in a series of self-destructive behaviors that she commits against herself and others. From carrying a concealed weapon, to fantasizing about killing her rapist, to committing arson, McDonald's rage nearly destroys her. Her narrative position shifts in much of section 2 of *Project Girl* due to her use of journal entries where readers are required to construct meaning on their own, rather than first-person narration where that power is located in the voice of the narrator. A direct telling through a protagonist-narrator's voice or a witness-narrator's voice gives the writer control over selecting what to tell and how to tell it; such a position, then, shapes the relationship between reader and author.

Narrative structure not only helps to frame, for readers, the state of mind of the author, but narration is also significant in the communication of ideological positions within a text. Roberta Trites explains, "How a text expresses its ideology is a function of narrative structure. The level at which ideology occurs affects the reader's perception of it."[13] If narration is constructed in first-person or third-person form, then the author has the choice to become part of the story or to remain outside of the story. *Project Girl*'s narrative structure shifts. Janet's first-person account of what led up to her emotional crisis is shaped by the only information she knows—her own lived experiences. Her telling of her own trauma communicates to readers the message that following trauma, there should be help in place for the victim lest she destroy herself. Gérard Genette terms this type of narrator an "extradiegetic narrator," or voices within the text that have a relationship with readers, or outsiders, of the text.[14]

The journal entries consist of Janet's internal conflicts, in which she blames both herself and the world for her problems. In deciding to include journal entries rather than first-person narrative based on them, McDonald creates a double-voice. The journal communicates ideologies about race, class, and gender. Readers are required to surmise Janet's progress in terms of her recovery, while at the same time, they must work to understand, through implicitly ideological positioning,

Janet's unraveling of the things that help and hinder her recovery. For much of section 2, Janet moves from a disaffective stance to a state of fury. Her journal entries match these polarities:

> I feel depressed, betrayed, ashamed, and most furious that I was raped and no one helped me, that I was overwhelmed at NYU and no one helped me, that I was wronged by the legal system, and no one helped me. Not family, not friends, not any shrink, not a soul. (*Project Girl* 139)

In section 3 of *Project Girl* McDonald returns to a linear narrative structure. Here, she takes the opportunity to wrap up the story of her early life. Section 3 is more centered and cogent than section 1 or 2. Readers travel with McDonald from her position as an associate in a law firm and the upper middle-class lifestyle that such a profession can provide, to Seattle, where she worked at a law firm, and eventually to Paris, where the memoir ends. The narrative structure in section 3 of *Project Girl* is in a familiar form to readers, and the journal segments in section 2 provide perspective so that section 3 will make sense to readers. In other words, had the journal entries been excluded from the narrative, there would be no explanation for Janet's continued emotional struggle.

The narrative alone serves as the subtext for a larger story about how no amount of success can take the place of self-acceptance. From the outside, McDonald's lawyer's suit, with a Burberry trench coat and Gucci shoes, was her masquerade as a portrait of success in the achievement of the American Dream. Internally, however, Janet possessed strong feelings of ambivalence regarding her own worth. Having gone through the trauma of rape, emotional distress, and time in jail, but yet graduating from several top universities is a major feat. The fact that Janet had achieved these milestones would have indicated that she should be in a constant state of elation, for she had surely beaten the odds. However, the emotional baggage of the trauma she suffered kept her off-track in finding a place where she could fit in. Instead, the trauma compounded her already present feelings of isolation. The daily grind of working in an environment where it was common for her to hear racial slurs and sexist rhetoric, the lack of self-esteem made her hours spent at work feel torturous. Residing at a posh address in Manhattan did not make her situation any better. However, living at an expensive address helped her develop the awareness and the eventual skills of addressing situations where she understood the unspoken rules about race and proximity, but refused to let those rules be hers. For instance, in her doorman-equipped apartment building, she was consistently asked, "May I help you?" whenever she appeared in the lobby. After several occasions of reminding the door person that she was, in fact, a resident of the building, she came to the point where she sternly let the staff know that she belonged in the building. After the incident, she was greeted with, "Good morning Ms. McDonald." This step to empower herself extended beyond her residence. She transferred that strength to situations at work where she stood her ground with fellow associates.

Furthermore, not only was McDonald's burgeoning sense of self surfacing in social and professional circles, but moments of self-actualization were also taking place from within. She recognized that most of her decisions were based on appearances. It was as if overcoming what she perceived to be her weaknesses with academic and career success would help to reconcile her feelings of worthlessness and shame surrounding having been raped. But no amount of success could assuage the anger and rage she felt over being attacked. McDonald explained:

> I wanted a little happiness and had begun to rethink my willingness, shared by most law-school graduates, to do anything that would "look good" on a resume. Up to that point in my life, I had bought the whole illusion: go to the right schools, work at the right firm, live in the right neighborhood in the right city. All those right moves have been wrong for me, and I wanted change. (*Project Girl* 221)

To that end, McDonald reconciled feelings of obligation to provide money for her family. The sense that she owed her family something had led her to spend much of her money on extravagances for her siblings and extended family. The realization that she was not obligated to provide such support freed her from guilt when she refused to lend money or purchase the latest fashions for her family. Coming to terms with the fact that she needed to create her own happiness was the starting point in McDonald's recovery from the trauma she had endured for nearly twenty years.

Janet's discovery that she was responsible for her own happiness was the catalyst for her move from New York to Seattle. No longer was she tied to the belief that working at a large New York firm signified her success. No longer was she so self-involved that she was unable to see the larger picture of how much of her displeasure with life rested on her refusal to accept her own reality. More than that, however, she came to terms with the fact that many of her problems centered around her quest to remain true to herself by possessing a clear picture of who she was. Instead, she seized whatever she perceived to be the things that created peace for others, and she drew a parallel to those things being able to work for her. For instance, smoking cigars, playing golf, and lunching with law partners are perfectly fine things to do, but when those things are done to gain acceptance, then disappointment will ensue. McDonald had to accept that her gender, race, and class did not keep her from living the life she desired, but those things do, in fact, matter in terms of self-acceptance. She could never be a white male golf-playing, cigar-smoking lawyer and such a situation is fine.

Seattle provided the space and time for her to get some perspective. She was able to cultivate real friendships because she turned her focus outward to see other people and their problems. She recognized that just as assumptions had been made about her in terms of her race and class, she had made the same assumptions about those unlike her. The sense that wealthy white children had it better than she did was challenged when, in Seattle, she was finally able to recognize the pain and anguish that can be suffered by virtue of family legacy. Where she worried about staying true to her roots and culture, she recognized that her white peers felt the pressure to measure up to the successes of their siblings and parents. The recognition that she could empower herself to make peace with the world made it possible for McDonald to begin her journey toward healing.

While some critics point out that the narrative structure of *Project Girl* detracts from the book's quality, others question whether or not McDonald responsibly reflects on the significance of the events that took place in her life. In a *Publishers Weekly* review, a critic challenges the level to which McDonald sorts out the impact of her drug use. Another reviewer criticizes the way in which she explores her psychological struggles.[15] At close examination though, McDonald provides important insight into the trouble that comes with not taking responsibility for one's actions. In the epilogue of *Project Girl*, McDonald writes, "My mistake was in my refusal to let my project-girl self evolve.

I confused evolution with substitution and was constantly fighting off some phantom 'white-girl' I feared would slip in during the night and substitute herself for me" (*Project Girl* 203). The battle against growth and change is what creates stagnation and grief. McDonald realized that her obsession with remaining true was really an obsession with fighting growth. Such a battle is hard fought and often lost. Readers travel with McDonald toward the realization that it is important to recognize how easy it can be to become one's own worst enemy.

Notes

1. Thomas Kennedy, "Up from Brooklyn: An Interview with Janet Mc-Donald," *Literary Review: An International Journal of Contemporary Writing* 44 (4) (Summer 2001): 704–20.

2. Janet McDonald, "Double Life," *Literary Review: An International Journal of Contemporary Writing* 45 (4) (Summer 2002): 679–84.

3. McDonald, "Double Life," *Literary Review: An International Journal of Contemporary Writing* 45 (4) (Summer 2002): 679–84.

4. Kennedy, "Up From Brooklyn."

5. Janet McDonald, interview by Catherine Ross-Stroud, Paris, France, March 13, 2007.

6. Geneva Smitherman, *Talkin' and Testifyin': The Language of Black America* (New York: Routledge, 2000).

7. Susan Tekulve, "Review of *Project Girl*, by Janet McDonald," *Literary Review: An International Journal of Contemporary Writing* 44 (4) (Summer 2001): 799.

8. Ross-Stroud interview.

9. Janet McDonald, *Project Girl* (New York: Farrar, Straus and Giroux, 1999), 107.

10. Ross-Stroud interview.

11. McDonald, *Project Girl*, 112.

12. Perry Nodelman and Mavis Reimer, *The Pleasures of Children's Literature*, 3rd ed. (Boston: Allyn & Bacon, c2003), 76.

13. Roberta Trites, *Disturbing the Universe: Power and Repression in Adolescent Literature* (Iowa City: University of Iowa Press, 2000), 70.

14. Gérard Genette, *Narrative Discourse: An Essay in Method* (Ithaca, NY: Cornell University Press, 1980).

15. "Forecasts: Nonfiction," *Publishers Weekly* 245, no. 47 (November 23, 1998): 28–29.

~

CHAPTER THREE

Real Project Girls:
A Literary Journey of Discovery

Following the critical acclaim of *Project Girl*, Janet McDonald felt a sense of pride for having tackled and completed the arduous task of writing a "real" book. She had initial thoughts of writing a sequel, as so many of her readers wanted to know more about the notorious project girl. *Paris Girl*, a tentative title for the second installment of *Project Girl*, had not gotten underway when it was suggested to McDonald by her agent that she try her hand at writing young adult novels. McDonald explains that her first inclination was to reject the idea of writing adolescent literature. She believed it to be "pseudo" literature and that adolescence, with its Sturm und Drang, tended to be trite and didactic. McDonald's dislike for adolescent literature was challenged when her agent also added that agreeing to write a young adult novel would mean an upfront payment of $10,000. McDonald explains that she accepted the challenge because "Who can afford to pass up that kind of money to do something that is fun and rewarding?"[1] However, she was apprehensive because she wanted to avoid those pedantic and preachy stories where the parents are at odds with the teens and, in the end, the adults in the novels have the last word, which is usually the "right" word for teen readers. So began the process of learning about and writing about teenagers. One of the first tasks at hand, then, was to actually read a young adult novel. McDonald, like many adults, and teachers in particular, had either not ever read a young adult novel or ceased to read them by the fifth or sixth grade. How, then, can these individuals assess the literary quality of a genre with which they are not familiar? In a monolithic view of adolescent literature, these books are often categorized as a set of Babysitters Clubs, Junior Harlequin Romances, and Nancy Drew Mysteries.

The point here is not to downplay the significance of series and formula novels. While young adults enjoy these novels, they also look for books that speak directly to them and comment on the meaningful things in their lives. Since young adult literature is assumed by some adults to be limited to one type of literary style and formula series are often predictable stories that rely heavily on plot rather than meaning, the conclusion is drawn that these texts offer no challenge for adolescent audiences. Donald Gallo responds most succinctly: "Complex does not necessarily equal greatness, nor does simplicity equal simple-mindedness."[2] Gallo goes on to explain that many of the same people who initially assumed that young adult literature consisted primarily of formula novels that are "one step above comic books" were surprised to discover the complexity and quality of adolescent literature. After having read several young adult novels, one educator in Gallo's discussion responded by saying, "I expected all these young adult books to be beneath my own reading repertoire as I supposed they were all 'juvenile' and 'immature fluff!' Wrong, wrong, wrong."[3]

McDonald began her search for literary substance with a hint of pessimism; to her surprise, however, she found herself mesmerized by the intensity of Holden Caulfield's self-absorption in J. D. Salinger's *Catcher in the Rye* (1951). The *Chocolate War* (1974), written by Robert Cormier, reminded McDonald of the social order of things in her own neighborhood of Farragut Homes. In Maureen Daly's *Seventeenth Summer* (1942), McDonald was bothered by the level of anticipation that Angela and Jack suffered. Like so many of my past and current students, McDonald wanted to know why Angela and Jack did not give in to their passions. McDonald read most of the "classic" and several contemporary young adult novels and had a serendipitous moment when, out of the haze of having read so many novels, it dawned on her that the early adolescent literature, while impressive in its own right, lacked diversity. While Angie and Jack showed the importance of postponement, Katherine and Michael, in Judy Blume's *Forever* (1975), communicated to their audiences that delayed gratification is overrated. McDonald expressed her dismay that black teens did not have a voice earlier in the genre. However, she appreciated the work of Walter Dean Myers and admitted that, like many young adult authors, her work is greatly influenced by his writing. Still, more needed to be done in terms of providing a forum for urban black teens who have beaten the odds. Sharon Flake's *The Skin I'm In* (1998) impacted McDonald in unexpected ways. The novel's protagonist is Maleeka, a dark-skinned adolescent female who lives in a single-parent home as the result of her father's death. Maleeka faces a series of problems: out-of-style clothing, a shy demeanor, and dark skin. Maleeka's self-esteem is almost nonexistent until she acquires a mentor, who helps her with self-acceptance. As a result, Maleeka is able to combat the social isolation she experiences because of her dark skin. McDonald's journey through adolescent literature brought her to the conclusion that while the characters do not have as much life experience as those in novels written for adults, they are likable and multidimensional. These works have the power to rescue or merely inspire young readers who are wrestling with similar issues. In short, McDonald was humbled by the power of young adult literature.

True to her belief that we must branch out to the unfamiliar in order for learning to take place, McDonald took up the challenge of constructing exceptional adolescent characters and situations. Creating characters and storylines that are unique, plausible, and free of stereotypes meant that McDonald needed to do a lot of research. She explained that her nieces were a good source of information for learning about teens, teen parenting, and becoming familiar with popular culture—music, clothing, and language.

Her first young adult novel, *Spellbound*, took about a month to complete. McDonald explained that since her law firm closed down for five weeks in late summer, she was able to spend about nine hours per day writing *Spellbound*. There were also those moments when, in the middle of her sleep, McDonald was awakened by the voices of her characters and was pulled out of bed by fear of losing these ideas. McDonald explained that some of those evenings turned into sleepless nights. By the end of the five-week recess from work, *Spellbound* was completed.

McDonald's goals for challenging herself to write realistic novels for all teens, particularly for black teens, was that she wanted to provide a voice for underrepresented identities in adolescent literature. While there are countless novels where the protagonists are white, middle-class, and male, she wanted to interject the voices of black teens who, on many levels, confront the same challenges as nonminority teens, but on another level, experience these challenges under different circumstances and in different settings.

Spellbound

The characters in *Spellbound* are familiar to many of McDonald's teen audience. Sixteen-year-old Raven Jefferson is an academically bright student who, like many teenagers, succumbs to the pressures of becoming sexually active before she is ready. Before her pregnancy, Raven's life in the projects is typical in that she is reared by a single mother who has a limited education and, thus, has had to grow up fast in order to confront the struggles that come with poverty. There is hope for Raven, however, because she has the potential to be academically and professionally successful like her older sister Dell, who is a paralegal at a Manhattan law firm. In the meantime, however, Raven must take responsibility for raising her newborn son on her own.

According to Barbara White, in her study of female characters in American literature, the construction of a character like Raven is logical in that novels that feature female adolescents share strong similarities with the author's life. In other words, "Adolescent novels obviously reflect the wide differences in the writers' individual circumstances—the age in which the author writes, the sections of the country where she lives, her political and social orientation, and her class and race."[4] While McDonald did not become a teenage mother, she witnessed the phenomenon in her community and also in her immediate family, as one of her sisters and several of her nieces became teen mothers. Also, the condition of being a welfare recipient as a contributing factor to the decline of the quality of life in housing projects is reflective of McDonald's experiences in Farragut Homes.

Thus, while it is important that authors of adolescent texts are mindful of the content in their work, it is also important to be aware of the realities that the implied readers of the texts face. The issue of plausibility matters just as much as creating a strong plotline. Furthermore, just as adults recognize the implausibility of characters they encounter in their reading, so do adolescents. Works with characters who are nothing like their readers have a slim chance of impacting the readers' lives. McDonald's mission was to create work that speaks to readers and gets them involved in the book. Authentic portrayals of life's realities are integral to the success of a novel, and success is measured first by the number of copies sold and checked out of libraries.

In order to balance her portrayal of urban project life, McDonald sought to reveal the richness of project communities as well. Within Raven's world, there is a sense of *communitas* that holds the families together. Raven's mother, although disappointed that her daughter is following in her footsteps by becoming a teen mother, is supportive of her daughter's desire to become more that just a teen mother on welfare. Similarly, Raven has a community of friends who support her mission of getting an education, a job, and a way out of the projects. One of these friends, Aisha, is also a teen mother, but she does not long for the same things as Raven does. Instead, Aisha prefers hanging out to going to school and does not care to get a job right away. While her goals are different from Raven's, Aisha babysits Raven's son, Smokey, while Raven is out searching for work, and when Raven begins to be depressed about her circumstances, it is Aisha who lifts her spirits with jokes and reminders that life will get better. Finally, McDonald infuses hope and redemption through her characters. Raven may be a teen mother, but she is smart and has a future in academia. While Aisha is not ambitious in the same way as Raven, readers see talents and generosity in her.

How Do You Spell Success?

Raven's search for a job lands her, not in an office as a secretary, as she would like, but in a fast food restaurant, Catfish Corner, which she dislikes. Raven's depression over her circumstances takes a toll on her self-esteem. Where once she felt hopeful that she could turn her life around, she begins to feel resigned to life in the projects. The job at Catfish Corner, however, turns out to be a blessing for Raven, because there she becomes reacquainted with Smokey's father, Jesse. One afternoon while Raven is preparing to close her register, a young man walks up to the counter and places an order. Raven immediately recognizes him as Jesse Honoré, the boy at the party in Hillbrook Homes a year ago who smooth-talked her into being intimate with him. Instantly Raven recalls all of her feelings of regret, anger, confusion, and abandonment. After the initial niceties of "I intended to call you" and "How long have you been working here?" Raven tells Jesse about the result of their one night together. Typical of these situations, Jesse questions Smokey's paternity and then quickly accepts Raven's assertions. He then promises to invite Raven to his house to meet his parents and to tell them about Smokey. Raven is doubtful that such a thing will happen, as Jesse is nervous about what his parents' reaction will be.

Coming from a middle-class family where his mother is a lawyer, his father is a high school principal, and his older sister is attending college, Jesse knows all too well how class-conscious his parents tend to be. Jesse feels pressure to measure up to his parents' expectations of success, which does not include becoming a teenage father to a baby, whose mother lives in a housing project. Jesse explains to Raven that when he told his parents about the baby, "They almost had a cow. . . . He [Jesse's father] said I might as well pack my bags if I thought I was bringing home . . . you know . . . a project baby" (*Spellbound* 175). The Honorés' response is a realistic portrayal of some parents' reactions to teen parenthood. The cycle of poverty that awaits many teen parents begins with the decision to be sexually active. Measures are not often taken to prevent pregnancy. Once the cycle of poverty begins, it is nearly impossible to escape.[5] While McDonald gives voice to the reality that many teens are sexually active, she does not overlook the fact that teens need to learn about the consequences of their decisions.

Many contemporary authors include storylines about black characters who are too young to marry or get a job, and so eschew the responsibilities of parenting. For instance, in Jacqueline Woodson's *The Dear One* (1991), fifteen-year-old Rebecca moves from her neighborhood in Harlem to the home where Feni, a middle-class suburban black teen, lives. Too young to marry, and not graduated from high school, Rebecca's future will consist of struggle and sacrifice to raise her baby. In most instances, the authors are careful not to judge the characters for their mistakes. Books like McDonald's confront this issue head on and with it, help readers understand a character such as Jesse. Like many adolescents, Raven and Jesse did not plan to be intimate nor did they intend to create a baby. Instead, McDonald's portrayal of these characters serves to show readers that teenagers are not as invincible as many teens believe themselves to be. At the same time, these characters demonstrate the innocence of adolescence—a cautionary tale for countless teens who may find themselves in the same predicament, because in the heat of the moment judgment has gone out of the window and risk has taken over. While there is a lesson to be learned from Raven and Jesse regarding proper decision making, there are also issues of family and future. Both families have significant internal bonds. Raven's mother and sister support her and the baby. Ms. Jefferson comforts Raven during difficult times and Raven's sister, Dell, instills hope by providing information about upcoming scholarships and educational programs that might fit Raven's circumstances. Jesse's parents, being more educated than the Jeffersons, demonstrate their commitment to family by applying pressure to succeed on their children. While these two families show the diversity that exists among black families, they all want the same things for their children: success, education, and happiness.

Prominent in *Spellbound*, too, is the issue of social and economic class. Project life and its by-products create challenges for residents, within and outside of their community. Both Raven's sister and Aisha's sister live in places other than Hillbrook Homes. Aisha's sister distances herself so much that she rarely comes to visit; Raven's sister, Dell, visits Hillbrook every week for Sunday dinner. While Dell is consistent with her visits, she is not always happy about having to visit her family in the projects. Dell's disdain for the project lifestyle becomes evident when, during each visit, she pokes fun at or criticizes Raven for something about project life. For instance, Dell points out to her sister that she is developing a "project girl booty," which means that, like many project girls, her behind is becoming so large that it is beginning to protrude outward. Dell's words communicate the feelings of many young adults who are in the process of integrating their past lives as project residents.

Pressures loom over Raven regarding class differences with Jesse and his middle-class parents. The Honorés are concerned that adding a member to the family who does not measure up to their standards in terms of family upbringing and lifestyle would have a negative impact on their quest for upward mobility. What is important to note, however, is that McDonald does not present Raven as being ashamed of her family's background. While Raven wants Jesse to be an involved father for their child, and at one point becomes distraught when she fears that Jesse will reject their son, never does she imply that because she lives in the projects she has less self-worth than those who do not. The elimination of the kid who feels bad because of growing up on the wrong side of the tracks is a step in the right direction in activating and maintaining a healthy concept of self.

Raven and Jesse's story serves as a backdrop for a larger issue concerning redemption. An overarching theme in McDonald's work centers around the belief that while people cannot start their lives over again, they can pick up where the mistakes end and get back on the right path. In this sense, Raven cannot change the fact that she has a baby, but she can finish her education to create a better way of life for her family. One mistake should not condemn us for life. Instead, McDonald communicates to her readers that hope, forgiveness, and perseverance have more to do with success than social status and unwise behavior.

Chill Wind

Chill Wind is the second installment of the Project Girls Series. Like *Spellbound*, *Chill Wind* focuses on a teen dropout mother who tries to get her life on track. As mentioned earlier, while *Chill Wind* can be read as a sequel to *Spellbound*, the novel can also stand on its own. The attention in this novel shifts from Raven Jefferson to Aisha Ingram, a nineteen-year-old unwed mother of two who receives notice that her welfare benefits will be cut off in thirty days. Unlike her best friend Raven who is ambitious, Aisha is content with sitting at home and chilling with her friends, watching television, and keeping up with the latest gossip. At first glance, it is possible for readers to compare Raven and Aisha and then conclude that Raven is a more likable character due to her desire to change her life for the better. However, Aisha is worthy of closer examination, especially since McDonald considers Aisha to be one of her favorite characters. McDonald thoroughly enjoyed writing Aisha's character because she possesses the personality traits that McDonald secretly wished for when she was a teenager: courage and bravado—even in moments when such an attitude is ridiculous. Even though Aisha's behavior is full of attitude with nothing to back it up, she is a likable character in that underneath her truncated speech and impulsiveness is a genuine person who takes care of those she loves. Aisha is wounded by her mother's drinking and inattentiveness, and so to compensate for feelings of vulnerability, she maintains an exterior of confidence and strength. Aisha, like many of McDonald's characters, is "at risk," in that she is what Sheila Anderson describes as an "extreme teen."[6] Anderson defines extreme teens as "those who are nontraditional in some way and who do not fit in the mainstream."[7] Anderson goes on to describe the various categories of extreme teens. Aisha fits several of these groups. She is a high school dropout; she is a teenage mother; she lives in poverty; and she lives in a single-parent home. All of these designations put Aisha at risk to becoming a productive citizen in society. Despite the fact that Aisha is in danger of being stuck in the cycle of poverty, she does not understand the gravity of her situation. Like many teens, Aisha is naïve because she does not look to the future nor does she reflect on the past; she lives for the moment, and when the moment changes, she reacts impulsively. Considering all of Aisha's negative qualities, then, why would McDonald include such a character? Borrowing from Donald Gallo's assertions that "Possibly the most important difference between the traditional classics and contemporary young adult novels is that YA novels help students feel normal, comfortable, and understood," Aisha's decision-making process is flawed just as that of some of the novel's readers.[8] Ask any teen if they have ever been in a situation where they made crazy and extreme decisions in order to solve a problem, only to discover later that their plans were comical, and many teens will answer, "Yes!" McDonald provides a comedy of errors to represent the extremes to which adolescents sometimes fail to think through their problems.

The humorousness of Aisha's attempts at solving her problems keeps teens laughing while it demonstrates to readers that she is not the clearest thinker when it comes to life's conflicts. For instance, believing in the unspoken ideology of an intact family as the way to survive, Aisha proposes marriage to the father of her children. She does so because proposing marriage would mean that she would have a husband to take care of her and the children, and thus she would be able to avoid getting a job. When her attempt at marriage fails, Aisha tries to convince the social service workers that she is mentally unstable. Of course such a move is not clever enough for the social workers, who have seen it all in terms of clients who want to avoid having their welfare benefits taken away. In both of these instances, readers get a sense of the immaturity that is still within Aisha. At the same time, readers see adolescent self-centeredness in the form of her behaviors. Aisha's struggle to avoid workfare is not a simple cautionary tale. McDonald is poking fun at some of the ideas that teens have about how their lives should work out for them. The sense of entitlement that Aisha conveys is a common theme in many teens' lives, as they are not always aware of how much work it takes to survive; they merely want things to work out.

Michael Cart explains that adolescent literature is popular among teens because it speaks to the very things that young adults worry about. Teens want to experience literature that validates their struggles. They want literature that does not pound them over the head with lessons. Often, it is better to show teens than to tell them. Cart mentions that the early adolescent "problem novel" was limited in its scope in that the principal worries of the teen characters in these early texts centered on drinking, drugs, and pregnancy. Contemporary novels do not stop at those issues. Young adults face more pressing issues today, and literature must reflect those problems. Still, young adult novels with their inclusion of contemporary problems, though useful for teens, often seem controversial to adults who want to protect young readers from these novels and their presumed power to "teach" readers a particular identity. McDonald, like many contemporary young adult authors, faces challenges based on the content of her works.

It might seem risky to not only include a storyline about teen mothers and welfare, but also a character who is defiant of authority and has an immense dislike for school and structure. However, Aisha's story is that of the prototypical adolescent character. According to Roberta Trites, one of the chief characteristics of an adolescent text is that "The protagonist must learn about the social forces that have made them what they are. They learn to negotiate the levels of power that exist in the myriad social institutions within which they must function, including family; school; the church; government; social constructions of sexuality, gender, race, class."[9] Added to Trites' assessment of proto-typical texts is the distinction made by Geta LeSuer. She suggests that the black female Bildungsroman is similar, yet distinct from the traditional version of that form in that the Bildungsroman written by black women authors "Seeks to discover, direct, and re-create the self in the midst of hostile racial, sexual, and other forms of societal repression."[10] A character such as Aisha conveys to readers not only the innocence of adolescence in terms of questing for power, but she represents the battles of ideological constructs that make her aware of her racial and gender oppression. At the same time, she both accepts and rejects the boundaries set for her by virtue of her race, class, gender, and age. Aisha accepts that she dislikes school and the sense of imprisonment that traditional education offers her. She comes to accept the fact that her days of "chilling" are coming to a close as the government controls her welfare benefits. She comes to accept that she is an unwed mother, and that such a situation means that she is alone to raise her children in a hostile society. However, Aisha does *not* accept that the decisions she made in the past preclude her grabbing the power to make her own choices about how she will survive in the future.

Aisha is not a follower, nor is she lazy. Not once in the text does Aisha assert that she does not want to become a productive citizen in society. Instead, her mission is to empower herself to choose a path that she can tolerate. The tension between her early life choices and the confining results of those decisions means that Aisha needs to be innovative in her quest to further herself. She cannot demand an office job or a college education, due to the fact that she is a high school dropout. She can, however, discover an alternative vocation to serving at fast food restaurants or working the subway patrol as a Workfare recipient. McDonald conveys to readers the importance of being creative and willing to persevere through tough situations. In Aisha's case, a modeling career with Big Models Inc. is the break that rescues her from the subway patrol job and potential homelessness. Critics question the plausibility of the novel's fairy tale–like ending. Nell Beram, for instance, writes, "This luck-dependent twist is disappointing, especially as it diminishes what seemed to be an emotional turning point: in an introspective moment, Aisha considers, ostensibly for the first time, that she might have had a big hand in her own bleak circumstances."[11] What Beram and others fail to recognize, however, is that McDonald's use of first-person narration provides a voice for the downfall that results from impulsive behavior and the quest to receive respect without first giving respect. While readers might be amused by Aisha's antics, those episodes are juxtaposed with characters such as Toya Larson, who provide alternative approaches such as continuing school and planning to marry before having children. McDonald's use of second-person narration to interject a discussion regarding the continuing trend of teenage pregnancy and its legacy of poverty is significant, in that teens such as Aisha enter the cycle of poverty without recognizing that on some levels, they are preconditioned to end up in the same situation as their parents, and that their early decisions are what will put them on this path. Moreover, McDonald helps readers understand that because the condition of poverty is so entrenched in everyday living situations, immunity to its warning signs makes it almost impossible to escape the reality.

Aisha, like Raven, presents to readers the possibility of change in the way that success is defined. Raven's path to success is conventional in the bootstrap tradition. Raven works hard, with the help of others, to pull herself up and out of the projects. The narrative of *Spellbound* focuses on the individual and the community, but ideologically, it is implied that readers view Raven as the key to her own success. Aisha's story, however, is the rags to riches tale that is prevalent in narratives of American success. Aisha is at the right place at the right time, and thus seizing serendipitous moments, coupled with her unfailing resolve to empower herself, is what makes her improved circumstances possible. At each step in Aisha's journey she encounters a person in a leadership role who tells her that "she has heart."[12]

Twists and Turns

The final novel in the Project Girls Series is *Twists and Turns*. Set in Hillbrook Homes, *Twists and Turns* chronicles the antics of Teesha and Keeba Washington, sisters who are experts at styling hair but struggle academically. The Washington sisters have a reputation for being the best braid stylists in their neighborhood, and as a result, their clientele skyrockets. Life goes on as usual for the Washington sisters as they attend school and braid hair in their spare time. However, things change once they finally graduate from high school. Keeba and Teesha realize that their partying days are numbered and that it is time to grow up. In fact, some of their best friends have already found success. Raven is engaged to Jesse Honoré and is away at college, Toya is enrolled in a computer course, and Aisha is a model for a major New York agency, Big Models Inc. In *Twists and Turns*, readers witness the impact that peer groups have on their friends. While Raven is the trailblazer of the group, being the first to branch out, Aisha follows not long after, which makes it only logical that the Washington sisters understand that their days of hanging out should be put to rest and replaced by responsibility and ingenuity.

Like *Spellbound* and *Chill Wind*, *Twists and Turns* asks, "What happens when you risk venturing out of comfortable surroundings?" McDonald's story answers the question: a sense of pride, growth, and a looking forward to the future happens. In *Twists and Turns*, the old adage "use what you have" rings true. The Washington sisters are not academically adept like Raven, and they are not impulsive and overly confident like Aisha. Instead, their talent lies in their ability to recognize their entrepreneurial potential. While this text is the third installment in a trilogy, readers do not have to be familiar with the two preceding novels in order to be captivated by the Washington sisters' story. While *Spellbound* and *Chill Wind* are often criticized for their fantasy endings, the conclusion of *Twists and Turns* is more plausible. In many high schools across the country, there are apprenticeship programs in place for girls like Teesha and Keeba, girls who are brilliant in their own way, but who need guidance and that extra push to use their talents to their advantage. However, while the ending of *Twists and Turns* is more realistic than those of the other novels in the series, the high drama, with political rallies, protests, crimes, and court scenes, is a bit dramatic. However, readers get the message, though heavy-handed, that nothing comes easy, but anything is possible with a lot of determination and community support.

The overarching theme of *Twists and Turns* centers on the myth of the self-made individual. In popular culture, there is Bill Gates and Sam Walton—all entrepreneurs who were not brilliant in their educational careers, but who grabbed an opportunity and ran with it.

These figures are larger than life, but their success sheds light on possibilities for Teesha and Keeba. An added element in McDonald's portrayal of the Washington sisters' climb to success as owners of TeeKee's Tresses is the reminder that the self-made individual, at close examination, gets help from somewhere. In the case of the girls, their community within Hillbrook Homes and people outside of their neighborhood support their endeavor. First Aisha lends the Washington sisters money to start up their business, then the community supports the Washington sisters by patronizing their business, which is located first in their apartment and then in a storefront in town. McDonald also takes a look at the importance of mentoring in the lives of adolescents, which can make the difference between success and failure—especially those adolescents who do not seek out traditional paths to success.

In the case of the Washington sisters, a college-educated young woman, Skye March, moves from her middle-class neighborhood to the Hillbrook Homes in order to be a role model for the teens in the housing complex. Skye's moving to Hillbrook is important in that her character demonstrates the significance of mentoring as a crucial element in changing the legacy of poverty. What is special about the inclusion of Skye in the novel is that, as in the first two installments of the trilogy, the Washington sisters are actively involved in their journey to success. McDonald is careful not to construct narratives where the characters are merely given blessings, such as wealth gotten from winning a lottery or from an inheritance or from convenient circumstances such as marrying well. Instead, the adolescent characters learn early on that it is necessary to be an integral part and not a bystander in changing one's life.

Such characters reflect McDonald's own life. For instance, while McDonald's admittance to prestigious schools was based on the acquisition of scholarship money, it was earned through her hard work and persistence. The struggle to upgrade her high school diploma from a vocational degree to an academic diploma was hard won, in that McDonald attended additional years of schooling to achieve her goal. While McDonald's Vassar education was funded by scholarships, she had to maintain her academic standing by struggling through the coursework while balancing her battles with personal demons. In each incidence, others around her who recognized her drive for success mentored Mc-

Donald. The careful interweaving of assistance and persistence is necessary, then, in helping young adult readers understand that nothing comes free. There is sacrifice and sometimes disappointment along the way. However, the resolve to achieve makes the struggles worthwhile.

McDonald also reminds readers that the quest for success does not end with the achievement of a particular goal. Instead, the cliché "It's lonely at the top" rings true. When Skye March helps redirect Keeba and Teesha's talents toward a more lucrative path by helping them open a hair salon, the Washington sisters are then faced with the dangers that come with success: jealousy and greed. Once TeeKee's Tresses is up and running, business is steady and profits are low, but things progress well until the landlords attempt to privatize Hillbrook Homes and thus increase the rent. Along with the possibility of financial ruin, the Washington sisters also have to confront the residual effects of peer group conflict, which brings with it an attempt to destroy TeeKee's Tresses by Shaniqua and Red, two project girls who seek revenge over the loss of a boyfriend. The salon is vandalized and almost set afire just as they are struggling to pay the rent that has doubled. The Washington sisters are uneasy about how to come up with the already high $400 per month rent when the owner of the building increases the amount, in order to force TeeKee's Tresses to close. Like most new businesses, TeeKee's Tresses is not profitable in its early stages, which worries Teesha and Keeba. Compounded by neighborhood gentrification and the displacement of the poor, the portrayal of the girls' success reveals the behind-the-scenes politics that hinder the quest for life changes.

The Importance of Place

The Project Girls Series was McDonald's first attempt at writing relevant fiction for teens. Because she has won several awards, most notably the Coretta Scott King/John Steptoe New Talent Award for *Chill Wind*, and has also been recognized by the American Library Association for her work, McDonald's attempts can be considered successful. Her success comes from not compromising what she has to say. Readers want the truth. Through the problems of the characters in the Project Girls Series, McDonald sheds light on how the shaping of identity has as much to do with the physical environment as it does with the emotional environment. Echoes of McDonald's mother's words—"You can take the girl out of the projects, but you can't take the projects out of the girl"—is an important theme in the Project Girls Series. Project Girl identity contains both subtle and overt characteristics, and these traits are embedded in project life as a whole. McDonald approaches the project girl identity with a twist, however, instead of the former pattern in which project life is portrayed as downtrodden and depressing.

For instance, readers might have seen the classic television show *Good Times*, in which the Evans family is confronted with a new dilemma in each episode. The portrayal of the close-knit and intact family is a positive aspect of the show, but the show's premise based on the life and struggles of the ghetto meant that readers did not get a sense of the Evans family's cultural traditions. Instead, Thelma and J. J. bantered while little brother Michael performed the role of the bookworm turned political radical. Rarely did viewers get to witness interaction with the other teens in the neighborhood—except in the context of negativity. While *Good Times* gave viewers insight into some of the struggles of living in poverty, the characterization of project life was lacking in its representation of project life's complexity.

McDonald's presentation of project life differs from *Good Times* and other texts dealing with ghetto life in that the adults speak of getting out of a supposedly horrid situation, while in McDonald's novels the young adults wrap their identity around their environment in order to make themselves whole. This desire to create a home is a necessary process in identity development because one of the first steps in identity formation is to ask the questions, "Who am I and where do I come from?" In popular culture project life is seen as an outlaw and rebellious designation. Just as McDonald had done at Vassar, the teens in the Project Girl Series use their project status in achieving their goal to define and be defined by their peers. One has to gain status from somewhere and that place can be located in roots in a housing project.[13] Positioning oneself as "project" for the young adults in the books carries with it the connotation of Anderson's extreme teen. The word speaks for itself. For instance, Dell's warning Raven that her behind is turning into a project girl's butt was mentioned without any further definition. Readers know what Raven looks like due to the lore of the projects in popular culture.

Teen Sexuality

Teen sexuality. Those words stir up a range of emotions for parents, teachers, and other adults who consider it their responsibility to protect children and teens from what is considered to be a faster-paced coming-of-age process these days. Nothing is new about this phenomenon, however. Instead, the push to protect our children comes from a heightened fear that if teens are exposed to anything that adults feel is inappropriate, then those teens will fall vulnerable to those influences. Teen sexuality is one area where this fear looms, although statistics in this area are hopeful. In a September 2006 report, written by the Henry Kaiser Family Foundation, it was reported that the rate at which teens are becoming sexually active has decreased from 53 percent of teens engaging in sexual activity to 47 percent. Of those teens, 91 percent of females and 83 percent of males report that they use some form of contraception when they engage in sexual activity. Finally, the pregnancy rate among teens is on the decline, with the rates falling from 117 pregnancies per 1,000 girls ages fifteen to nineteen in 1990 to 84 in 2000. While the Kaiser Report can be taken as good news for society as a whole, those statistics remain rather high. Based on the Kaiser Report, it is no wonder that adults are concerned about teens and their blossoming sexuality.

Adolescent novels that contain references to sexual activity or portrayals of teen pregnancy are often challenged for their content. However, McDonald's treatment of the subject neither glorifies nor vilifies. Instead, her depiction of teen sexuality in the Project Girl Series is rather detached from the larger issue of personal achievement. McDonald's portrayal of teen sexuality as a marginal issue is similar to that in the narrative of her memoir, *Project Girl*. Like the memoir, these girls have problems that go beyond a discussion of sexual engagement. Perhaps McDonald felt it more important to focus on solutions to the problems the girls face, as the cause is quite obvious. Furthermore, taking into consideration Roberta Trites' assessment of the depiction of teens' sexuality in adolescent novels, "Adolescent literature is as often an ideological tool used to curb teenagers' libido as it is some sort of depiction of what adolescents' sexuality actually is"[14] In this sense, McDonald's work does not address teen sexuality in terms of society's ideological position. It could be argued, however, that McDonald should take up the issue in a way that makes the dangers of teen sex clear to her readers. Such cautionary tales, however, already exist in countless young adult novels.

On the other hand, while the Kaiser Report reveals a decrease in sexual activity among teens in general, still 68.8 percent of African American teens surveyed revealed that they have engaged in some form of sexual activity. This number is steep compared to other groups such as Latino and white, who collectively average in the fiftieth percentile. Granted, these data are skewed, in that the numbers do not represent all teens in America. However, with such a large percentage, perhaps some sort of antisex statement could quell the voices of censors, but a corrective voice in adolescent literature will serve mostly to deter readers instead of converting them.

McDonald plays around with the notion of teen parents and marriage when Aisha, in an act of desperation, proposes to the father of her children. She addresses the clichéd notion of boys only wanting "one thing" from girls with Raven and Jesse. In each instance, readers come to recognize McDonald's ideological position about teen sex. Her novels do not resort to the didactic storyline that novels conclude with a depressed teen mother who regrets her past decisions. McDonald's characters learn to forgive themselves for their mistakes and then right their wrongs by getting back on track. McDonald depicts teen sexuality as a minor concern, and she provides characters who are from the projects who do not get pregnant. In *Twists and Turns*, the Washington sisters take longer than most students to graduate from high school because they were held back a few grade levels. However, they stick with school and manage to graduate without the extra baggage of parenting. McDonald seems to be saying to readers that not all project girls get pregnant and receive welfare as the stereotypes suggest.

Race and Those Loud Black Girls

Novels that focus on black girls who are sexually active and on welfare are dangerously close to reinforcing stereotypes. The need for black authors to represent blackness at its finest, rather than in degrading images, means that McDonald's choice of project girl characters requires care in the progression of the narrative and the outcome of the story. McDonald's personal insight into the project girl identity helps to balance a realistic portrayal of project life with the depiction of people who fit the harmful stereotypes that are attached to black women. While Raven and Aisha are teen mothers, they are not identical in their approach to problem solving. And although both girls receive welfare, neither sees poverty as a way of life. McDonald's careful consideration of the negative images of black women in the media and beyond is a crucial element in the success of the novels. The protagonists of the Project Girl Series are taken seriously because they are portrayed in a way that moves beyond the angry black girl myth. Because McDonald creates sensitive and intelligent characters, readers are able to see the vulnerabilities that come with growing up female. Thus, while Aisha is sometimes loud and abrasive, readers come to understand her behavior at other points in the narrative. While Raven can be read as naive, readers witness her strength and knowledge as she fights her way from high school dropout to college co-ed. In less contemporary novels, black characters are often presented as one-dimensional. McDonald's work depicts these types of characters as complicated individuals, and so gives them more credibility to readers.

Notes

1. Janet McDonald, interview by Catherine Ross-Stroud, Paris, March 13, 2007.
2. Donald Gallo, "Listening to Readers: Attitudes Toward the Young Adult Novel," in *Reading Their World: The Young Adult Novel in the Classroom*, ed. Virginia Monseau and Gary Salvner (Portsmouth, NH: Heinemann, 1992), 25.
3. Gallo, "Listening to Readers," 25.
4. Gallo, "Listening to Readers," 25.
5. Jason DeParle, *American Dream: Three Women, Ten Kids, and a Nation's Drive to End Welfare* (New York: Viking, 2004).
6. Sheila Anderson, *Extreme Teens: Library Services to Nontraditional Young Adults* (Westport, CT: Libraries Unlimited, 2005), 5–6.
7. Anderson, *Extreme Teens*, xix.
8. Gallo, "Listening to Readers," 25.

9. Roberta Trites, *Disturbing the Universe: Power and Repression in Adolescent Literature* (Iowa City: University of Iowa Press, 2001), 10.

10. Geta LeSeur, *Ten is the Age of Darkness: The Black Bildungsroman* (Columbia: University of Missouri Press, 1995), 110.

11. Nell D. Beram, "Chill Wind," *Horn Book* 78 no. 1 (January–February 2002): 80.

12. Janet McDonald, *Chill Wind* (New York: Farrar, Straus and Giroux, 2002).

13. Jeff Chang, *Can't Stop Won't Stop: A History of the Hip-Hop Generation* (New York: St. Martin's Press, 2005).

14. Trites, *Disturbing the Universe*, 85.

CHAPTER FOUR

~

Harlem Boys:
Brother Hood and *Harlem Hustle*

In the Brother Hood novels, McDonald introduces us to male protagonists, Nathaniel "Schoolie" Whitely and Eric "Hustle" Samson, two black teens born and raised in Harlem. The Brother Hood books are a departure from McDonald's usual focus on project girls in Brooklyn. Both *Brother Hood* and *Harlem Hustle* are unique in that, although the boys are the focus of the work, New York, in general, and Harlem, in particular, are characters as well. These novels expose teens to books, ideas, and facts that they otherwise would not encounter on their own. At the same time as McDonald introduces readers to worlds different from their own, she also tackles some of the pressing issues that teens, black teens in particular, encounter on a daily basis. In *Brother Hood* Nathaniel Whitely is a promising student who grows up and is educated in Harlem's public schools but earns a scholarship to the prestigious Fletcher School in upstate New York. Hustle's path is different. He is an abandoned teen who turns to the streets for survival. While Nate spends time studying the classics at Fletcher School, Hustle spends his time dodging jail. The tie that binds these two characters is their friendship. Nate and Hustle are childhood buddies who understand each other's differences. Their relationship is in contrast to the tensions that black teens typically face when one is school oriented and the other finds success through other modes.

McDonald explained that she received a constant stream of e-mails and letters from readers who wanted to read about male characters. They asked her to set her stories in other places besides projects. These readers are in search of a voice that is representative of their experiences, too. McDonald obliged her readers by providing the Brother Hood novels, but with a twist. The characters in these novels are meant to be plausible, while at the same time hopeful. McDonald does not ignore the realities of urban life with its race and class prejudice. She does not ignore the need that readers have to see characters succeed through nontraditional means other than drug dealing. There is also an acknowledgement that within the urban setting, there exist close ties to community and a commitment to family; as a result, images of family and familylike relationships are prevalent in her work. Also, while McDonald feels that it is important to maintain the racial identity of the characters in her books, she also seeks to contest commonly held racial and ethnic stereotypes, in order to expose readers to a range of definitions of what it means to come of age as a teen in America. McDonald explodes numerous myths and stereotypes pertaining to urban youth and urban living. Harlem becomes not the mythical place of early twentieth-century prosperity and later twentieth-century decline. Harlem is alive with its people. The question becomes, then, how are survival and success possible in an environment that is challenged by its race and its history?

The Souls of Nathaniel

Double-consciousness is a common theme in adolescent literature and in *Brother Hood* Nathaniel Whitely divides his time between the Fletcher School and his home in Harlem. Readers are immediately introduced to Nate's struggle with duality as the novel opens with his traveling to Harlem while reading Fyodor Dostoevsky's literary classic, *Crime and Punishment*. Surrounded by several of his schoolmates, Nate is consumed by the novel and so is not aware of his surroundings. However, once he arrives at Grand Central Station, he transforms himself from a prep school student to a brother from the hood. The space between the two designations is not vast in that Nate's academic ability has been a part of his identity from the start of his school career. At the same time, however, Nate does not socially isolate himself from his friends who do not care for school in the same way he does. Thus, the theory of "acting white" is a myth that McDonald explodes right away. In none of Nate's interactions with his friends is he chastised for his concern for education.[1] At the same time, Nate does his part by changing his clothing before he arrives in Harlem in order to demonstrate his solidarity with his community, not because he will be harassed if he wears his Fletcher uniform, but because he wants to leave school behind temporarily so that he can be a full member of his home community. Furthermore, the issue of double-consciousness is important to mention here as well. Nate's attendance at Fletcher School does not change his level of awareness about the impact of race, gender, and class on his coming of age. Nate is keenly aware of the differences in the reactions he gets when he switches outfits. He knows that the comfort level of fellow train passengers shifts depending on his appearance. A black male sporting a prep school uniform is far less menacing to some than his Harlem gear complete with a do-rag. In this sense, Nate's power to code switch via physical appearance makes a personal and also a political statement about his identity.

Researchers (White, 1998; Crane, 2000; Dyson, 2005) argue that clothing, especially for those members of society who feel the pressure of race, gender, and class oppression, becomes a vehicle of empowerment. In Crane's (2000) study of the historical legacy of personal expression through fashion, she explains that as early as the nineteenth century, oppressed groups (women, blacks, ex-slaves) assembled outfits that conveyed the contradictory nature of their given political status.[2] For instance, women would combine a male suit coat and necktie with a corseted dress or hoop skirt. Similarly, blacks of lower classes adorned themselves in clothing of the white upper class in order to communicate an appearance of having more resources than what was actually available to them. In each of these instances, the awareness that the clothing would not change their status in a true sense, however, the motivation for sporting such clothing combinations served as an act of rebellion against the power hierarchies that existed within their community—a type of border crossing, so to speak. Contemporary fashion, while less rigid than nineteenth-century sensibilities, is still circumscribed by a set of unspoken rules.

Class and gender are the most-often recognized domains of personal expression through fashion. Simple, nondescript styles of dress are often associated with middle- and upper-class fashion while flashy and extreme combinations are associated with working class and poor groups. In the case of Nate, his style of dress communicates several levels of class and gender distinctions. Coupled with the change in his walk from a casual stroll to a sort of strut to mark his masculinity, the baggy jeans, the big shirt, and the do-rag mark his self-situated place in the category of urban and working class. This combination, coupled with the gender and race of the wearer, ignites fear in those who buy into race, gender, and class stereotypes regarding this style of dress. Nate then uses clothing to self-designate himself into whatever group he desires to be associated with at a given time.

Dyson (2005) would argue that Nate's style, ghetto couture or ghetto chic, is linked to the controlling of one's identity. Deciding to wear ghetto couture-style clothing, even with the knowledge that this particular style is associated with violence and crime in that when incidences of crime are described by the media, the suspect's attire is often described as that of ghetto couture, is an act of empowerment for the wearer similar to calling attention to oneself as being a member of a nonconventional culture. In fact, Dyson (2005) asserts that while the origin of oversized clothing for instance is linked to prison attire and prison life, "Most youth who wear baggy jeans and oversized shirts are probably not even aware of their origins, and when they find out are not likely to give up the fashion because its beginnings don't determine the use of the style. Many black youth who wear baggy pants may feel they are already in prison, at least one of perception, built by the white mainstream and by their dismissive, demeaning elders" (*Is Bill Cosby Right?* 117–18).[3] Resistance to fashion conformity is one of only a few ways to empower oneself without suffering legal consequences. Ask any black teen about what it means to act white and you will hear several descriptions. Some teens will mention clothing, others music, while many will describe one's choice of friends and social networks as deciding factors on whether one is acting white. The common belief that black teens merely equate acting white with academic achievement is a myth. View any talk show or read any article about acting white and witness, that while a circuitous discussion might take place regarding the topic, the one parallel that is often drawn is that connection between black teens and their alleged commitment to anti-intellectualism.

Research studies have been conducted on the topic of the acting white phenomenon and black teens' commitment to educational achievement. In his groundbreaking study, the late John Obgu explored the achievement gap of black teens from a middle-class Ohio suburb. While the project is an exploratory study of the root causes of low achievement among black middle-class students, one common thread in his findings addresses the acting white theory. Ogbu's study supports the premise that the notion of anti-intellectualism among black teens exists.

However, Angela Neal-Barnett and Robert Stadulis's 2007 study challenges the claims of these researchers. In their exploration of the acting white phenomenon, they discovered that black teens define acting white more broadly. Instead of academic performance being the deciding factor, Neal-Barnett and Stadulis's results confirm that black teens, if asked directly, will share that clothing, speech, social networks, and outside interests are indicators. Moreover, the study results reveal that, because the belief in the anti-intellectual theory is so embedded in our ideological constructions of black adolescence, black students who are accused of acting white often respond to this indictment by identifying their achievement as the cause of their social isolation, and thus begin to revert to low-level achievement and rebellion. Even black students buy into the damaging stereotypes regarding race and scholastic commitment.

Furthermore, when Neal-Barnett and Stadulis surveyed white students regarding characteristics of acting black, they listed categories such as form of dress, speech, one's gait, and music tastes. When queried regarding their definition of acting white, these students could not formulate a response. Neal-Barnett and Stadulis assert that this "suggests that even white adolescents have adopted the black definition of being white."[4] Forgoing research results that reinforce socially constructed definitions of being black and adolescent, McDonald chose instead to provide readers with an array of characters who represent the diversity of identities among black teens.

One thread that ties the Brother Hood Series together is the fact that McDonald does not create scenes in her novels that focus on intraracial chiding regarding academic performances. The adolescents in her novels are rarely judgmental of each other's academic or professional endeavors. Perhaps McDonald's decision to forgo the tendency for black characters in novels to address anti-intellectualism as a positive character trait has much to do with her experiences as a developing academic. As we have seen, McDonald's fiction is highly autobiographical on some levels. McDonald is careful in all of her books to avoid constructing characters that are not supportive of one another's dreams. At the same time, McDonald is also careful to make sure that the characters who take traditional roads to success are offset by those characters who are not so conventional in their quest for success.

Realism enters into Nate's story when readers meet his family. The Whitely family is comprised of his married parents, who maintain their family and home with working-class jobs, and an older brother, Eli. The parable of the prodigal son enters into McDonald's narrative in that Nate and Eli are foils of each other in terms of ethics and education. While Nate is studious, Eli drops out of high school. Where Nate is law abiding, Eli is not. Instead, while they love Eli, the Whitely family is frustrated by the decisions he makes. For instance, Eli invades the territory of other neighborhood criminals in his quest to pick up more clientele for his number-running (gambling) business. The Whitelys constantly worry about their own and Eli's safety because all of the Whitelys could be hurt from the choices that Eli makes. While his family tries to stick by him, Eli does not give them consideration in return. Instead, he operates as if he is not connected to his family in any way. Eli demonstrates his lack of loyalty toward his family when he visits Nate's girlfriend, Shantay, while Nate is away at school.

McDonald's intention is not to make Nate look good while making Eli look bad. Instead, Eli's narrative is a reflection of reality. In families with multiple siblings, it is common that at least one child goes astray. Eli's story is McDonald's method of "keeping it real" for her readers.[5] At the same time McDonald is careful to balance her narratives so that none of her characters, especially the black ones, turn out to be mere stereotypes.

Nate's Double Life

At Fletcher School, Nate plays lacrosse; in Harlem, Nate plays basketball. At Fletcher, Nate wears a coat and tie; in Harlem, Nate wears a do-rag, long T-shirt, and baggy jeans. The common denominator for Nate, then, is that his sense of himself is intact in both locations. Nate does not fall into the pattern of focusing on his blackness to the degree that his thinking gets in the way of his progress. Instead, Nate understands the dynamics of race in a way that keeps him grounded in the knowledge that, although he is privileged as a prep school student, and the prep school status affords him a few allowances, he is also a black male in America and that means that his race is the indicator most often used by nonminorities to rank his status in society. For instance, when Nate and his best friend Hustle are arrested for a traffic violation, Nate does not expose Hustle's wrongdoings to get freedom for himself. Instead, with the mission of getting back to school on time, Nate discloses to the police that he is a prep school student; the information is verified and he is let go. Because of Nate's social awareness, he knows what information to disclose about himself and at what moment the disclosure should happen.

Nate Whitely's character type is not new to young adult literature. He is the dualistic teen who is painfully aware of his two lives. The difference between Nate's character and the other characters who are a part of this narrative is that by the end of the novel, Nate fares well. For instance, classic novels such as J. D. Salinger's *Catcher in the Rye* (1951) and John Knowles's *A Separate Peace* (1959) contain characters that, by the end, are in distress. In terms of black adolescent literature, novels such as Jacqueline Woodson's *Maizon at Blue Hill* (1992) and Martha Southgate's *The Fall of Rome* (2002) portray black students who experience distress in their elite prep school environment. Maizon is a bookish twelve-year-old who wins a scholarship to attend suburban Connecticut's Blue Hill Academy. Maizon arrives by train at her new school only to discover that she is out of her league socially because she is from a working-class neighborhood in Brooklyn, where she lives with her grandmother. Maizon is so overwhelmed by her perceived underclass status that she is unable to perform scholastically. In the end, the pressure is too great, and so she decides to return to Brooklyn and attend her old school where she feels comfortable. Woodson's portrayal of a character who gives up so soon does not necessarily send an empowering message to her readers. In *The Fall of Rome*, Rashid Bryson is an urban teen who enrolls in an elite New England boarding school for boys. Along with Rashid's other belongings, he brings to school the baggage of his life, which includes anger over the random shooting and subsequent death of his older brother Kofi. Rashid struggles with his classes, especially his classical literature class, where he has the most trouble. The instructor of the course, Jerome Washington, one of only a few blacks on the campus, criticizes his work and attempts to fail Rashid altogether. The conflict between Rashid and Washington comes to a head when the teacher gives Rashid an unfair failing grade on an assignment. The situation escalates when Washington slaps Rashid, thus ending his career as a teacher at the prep school.

Stories such as those mentioned above serve a particular purpose for their readers. McDonald's interjection of Nate's voice adds another dimension to the traditional school story. Nate is comfortable in his skin. He does not boast of his street knowledge to his school peers nor does he distance himself from his Harlem peers. McDonald's own experiences with adjusting to unfamiliar surroundings did not go as smoothly as Nate's. Due to her emotional turmoil, McDonald was not able to concentrate on her studies.

Instead, she obsessed about her surroundings and how the Vassar environment was not meant for her. At one point in her Vassar career, McDonald described the moment when a professor assigned a writing task to the class. While the other students were able to write about their travels to Europe and their hobbies, McDonald wrote about life in the projects. To her dismay, she received a bad grade and was told that her work did not fit the creative writing assignment. Instead, said the teacher, her piece represented a sociological point of view. Such a move by an instructor was a defining moment for McDonald. Just as she had had to reorient herself to fit the protocols of Erasmus High School, she discovered that the same task was needed to survive at Vassar. Thus, Nate's comfort with academic subjects and his participation on the school's lacrosse team is the antithesis of McDonald's experiences in a suburban academic setting.

At the same time, Nate's ability to integrate himself into his neighborhood is the opposite of McDonald's experience in Farragut Homes. McDonald did not understand that she could be both a school girl and a project girl. The character of Nate represents McDonald's reconciliation of her own warring duality. Reviewer Hazel Rochman, however, questions McDonald's portrayal of Nate. She asserts, "He's just too perfect, and the message about a successful kid who doesn't reject his roots is overstated." No matter how unreal Nate's adjustment appears to readers, it is important that McDonald include a narrative that demonstrates how, while racism and classism exist everywhere, teens do not have to take on the negative energy of such beliefs. Instead, as McDonald shows readers, it is important to be aware of racist beliefs, because the knowledge is empowering to readers in that they are not surprised by racism and classism, nor are they victims.

Social Networks as Support against Racism
Along with Nate's comfort with traveling between his two worlds, school and home, is the portrayal of his social networks. Nate has friends in both locations and these friendships are depicted as nearly perfect; underneath, however, these friendships are more complex. To begin with, Nate's good friend at Fletcher School is Spencer. Spencer is a WASP from a wealthy family who is also a known drug dealer on the Fletcher campus. The nonwhite students recognize that Spencer has privileges that are not afforded to them. One of those privileges is that, while everyone knows Spencer sells drugs, he is not suspended from the lacrosse team nor is he kicked out of school. In one scene, Willa, Nate's girlfriend at Fletcher, reflects on the double standard when it comes to school rules.

At one point in the novel, Spencer challenges Nate's assumptions about race and class. At first Nate assumes that Spencer is a WASP. He learns that his family's last name is Adamowicz and that "my (Spencer's) grandfather changed his last name when he left Poland right before the war. We're Jewish. We reinvented ourselves" (*Brother Hood* 78). This scene is a weak moment in the novel, because McDonald does not have Spencer and Nate further deconstruct the complexity of race surrounding the issue of immigrants who hold the privilege of disassociating themselves from a marginalized or oppressed group.

Although McDonald does not provide analysis of racial privilege in *Brother Hood*, she does expose readers to instances of interracial prejudice. For instance, when Fletcher's lacrosse team plays in a match against Drucker Prep, Nate is brutalized on the field by several of the Drucker players. The tension between the two teams mounts until a brawl ensues. Later that evening, Spencer and Nate reflect on the day's events. Because Nate was assaulted so badly, Spencer jumped in and defended him, which led to a two-game suspension for Spencer. Nate questions Spencer's motives, to which Spencer explains, "I know you can take a wallop . . . but there are some jerks on the Druids team who deliberately go after non-wasps . . . Blacks, Catholics, Chinese, Jews, it doesn't matter to these jerks" (*Brother Hood* 76). Spencer's revelation about being Jewish gives Nate some perspective for his reasons for defending him on the field, but Nate's response to the entire situation is implausible.

To begin with, Nate responds to Spencer's assertions that the Druids are racist by remarking, "Hey, it's a rough game. Everybody takes a beating" (*Brother Hood* 76). Nate continues to reflect on his experiences at Fletcher and concludes that "Other than a bad vibe here or a slight attitude there, nothing racial had come up since he'd been at Fletcher. The place was pretty cool, even if most of the students were white and come from money" (*Brother Hood* 77). While it can be argued that McDonald constructs this scene in order to communicate to readers the pitfalls of focusing on their race as the cause for problems they might have in school, it is unrealistic for McDonald to expect readers to find Nate's words believable. In this sense, McDonald had the perfect opportunity to address the complicated issue of racism while, at the same time, creating a character who is able to go beyond race. Such a move creates contradictory images of the politically and racially aware Harlemite and the naïve prep schoolboy.

While her portrayal of Nate's social understanding is lacking in terms of race within his school setting, McDonald is adept at depicting Nate's ability to unravel the intricacies of intraracial classism and prejudice. One of the few black students on the Fletcher campus is Nate's friend Willa. Nate struggles with his relationship with Willa because he is also in a committed relationship with Shantay, his "round-the-way-girl" from Harlem. Shantay and Willa are foils of each other in that Shantay's identity is cultivated by way of Harlem's standards of hip-hop culture, while Willa is an upper-middle-class girl from the suburbs. When Nate invites Willa to an outing in Harlem, Willa agrees, but with reservations. Once in Harlem, Willa is overwhelmed by the culture of fashion with its do-rags and baggy jeans. She is put off by the slanglike speech that the teens use, and she resents being objectified by teenage boys around her. Willa is especially surprised, however, when she meets Hustle, Nate's best friend. Nate's two worlds collide when Willa demands allegiance from Nate in her quest to separate herself from the Harlemites and Nate is determined to acknowledge his friends and represent his neighborhood.

As a result, Willa is rude to Nate's friends and even insults one by saying "and I suppose *Double Fo* stands for two 4's as in forty-four magnum? Very trite, actually. Every boy-in-the-hood movie has some loser named for a gun" (*Brother Hood* 114). When Nate asks Willa to "chill out," she says, "What is so real about speaking bad English? Do your hoodlum friends go to school? Do they have futures? I think I don't know you very well at all . . . *Schoolie*" (*Brother Hood* 115). The scene closes with Nate standing with his friends and wondering what to do next.

McDonald's portrayal of the social class divide between lower-class blacks and middle-class blacks is realistic. The terms *buppy*, *boojee*, and *bourgeois* are thrown back and forth between the various classes of blacks.[6] Depending on the context, one can perform a different class identity, but only so far. For instance, Nate is adept at code-switching to the point where his speech and his affect are not overtly lower class. Once in Harlem, Nate is able to switch back and forth between his school protocols and his home behaviors. It is as if the ability to turn these two worlds off and on is a necessary skill for Nate and readers like him. Since the tendency is to view higher socioeconomic status as the standard in our society, the ability to avoid having a clear preference for one over the other is necessary. Nate's support of his Harlem peers is a risky move, in that he must return to Fletcher where perhaps his family background might affect his reputation. If Nate acts as if he is surprised by Spencer's telling him about the Druid team, we can conclude that Nate sees himself as a member of Fletcher first and black second. Nate has managed to garner his self-esteem from his ethnic and social position rather than his economic status.

Willa's reaction to Harlem and its people tells a different story. Her remarks regarding bad English and urban teen behavior communicate to readers that her self-esteem comes from her socioeconomic status rather than her allegiance to a city or a particular racial group. Willa is able to distance herself from the black community by virtue of her parents' money.

Harlem Hustle: A Transformation in Words

Harlem Hustle is McDonald's second installment in the Brother Hood Series. The protagonist, Eric Samson, is a turn away from McDonald's usual character types. Eric "Hustle" Samson is an orphaned teen with a police record. While all of McDonald's characters struggle with their life's circumstances, Hustle is the first of her characters to have official contact with the legal system. Eric's drug-addicted parents abandoned him, so as a means of survival, he turns to the streets where he boosts (steals) trendy clothing and then sells it at a reduced price to his friends and to customers he encounters on the streets. Eric spends his childhood being passed around from one relative to another until he finally ventures out on his own. Although Hustle commits crimes in order to survive, McDonald does not portray his actions as appropriate or necessary. Instead, through Eric, McDonald takes the opportunity to expand her readers' horizons by having them witness Eric's growth. *Harlem Hustle*, then, is a book that takes on many aspects of coming-of-age and is an exploration of hope, family, and knowledge in the context of Hustle's struggles.

In the beginning of the novel, Hustle is in a Times Square clothing store where he commits many of his boosts. Having recently been caught shoplifting Hustle is insecure about his ability to spot the five-o (police). While he is trying on potential items to be stolen, a group of girls enter the store, which makes him lose his concentration. Hustle gives up on shoplifting for a moment in order to speak to the girls. However, the girls stage a flirtation in order to pick his pocket. In this scene readers are immediately introduced to the problems that come with criminal activity. McDonald makes us aware that a life of crime is a life where one can be both the culprit and the victim of theft, and in both positions there is loss. Hustle's predicament is doubly bad in that there is no one to whom he can confide that he has been robbed; his masculinity will not allow it. Instead, Hustle shakes off the discovery that his wallet has been stolen by a group of girls.

To open an adolescent novel with a description of criminal activity may seem risky; however, McDonald situates her readers directly in the midst of their reality. Knowledge of boosting clothing is common in adolescent circles and especially so in urban areas where there are plenty of shops and idle, jobless teens. Picking pockets is a common occurrence among urban dwellers. What makes this scene necessary, then, is twofold. Urban adolescent readers, McDonald's implied audience, and teens in general are in search of books that accurately represent their world—even if the portraits are unsettling to adults. Furthermore, scenes such as these are effective literary devices in that they capture readers' attention, especially reluctant readers who tend to gravitate toward action-filled narratives. McDonald's inclusion of these occurrences evidences her understanding of teen life and its pitfalls.

The scenes in the first chapter set the stage for the everyday life of urban teens: those who get arrested multiple times and run out of aliases and thus are found out, the "fast" girls whose parents come searching for them out of fear that they could be getting into situations that they will regret, and the buzz of energy that comes with the confusion of adolescence. Entangled with this adolescent angst is music. McDonald presents the reality of loss to her readers, but infuses hope by giving Hustle the gift of his music; he is an aspiring rap artist who, throughout the novel, transforms his lyrics from inappropriate rhymes such as "Back seat shorties who know how to be naughty" to socially responsible lyrics that challenge anti-intellectualism and violence among teens. In Hustle's struggles, readers understand the power of perseverance and the possibility of change and, at the same time, readers get a few history lessons.

The Revolution Will Not Be Televised
Growth and change is a theme within *Harlem Hustle*. Just as we witness Hustle's growing trust in other people, we also see the words of his songs change from sexually explicit lyrics to more socially conscious songs that speak out against misogyny, violence, and anti-intellectualism. Given the current state of hip-hop culture, with its challenge to artists to take into consideration their work's impact on their audiences, it is no surprise that McDonald takes up this issue. Hustle's girlfriend, Jeannette

Simpson, introduces him to her grandmother, Nanna. Once she learns that Hustle is a wannabe rapper, Nanna asks Hustle to demonstrate his talent. He recites the words to his recently written lyrics:

> She was a back seat shorty, know how to be naughty
> Bust her out she cry lawdee
> Bust her out she want more-dee. (*Harlem Hustle* 78)

Throughout his recitation of the lyrics, Hustle does not notice Nanna's growing discomfort. Instead, his lack of a formal upbringing means that he does not have a clear social awareness regarding respect for elders and the use of appropriate language around adults. Embedded in the humor of this scene is McDonald's awareness of some of the social issues that teens encounter. Despite Hustle's faux pas, Jeannette is able to convince Nanna to give Hustle another chance. Nanna, a schoolteacher, takes on the duty of helping to socialize Hustle. One of the first areas that Nanna works on with Hustle is his habitual use of incorrect grammar. Similarly, Nanna challenges Hustle about the content of his lyrics. Nanna becomes the voice of many people who are concerned with the demeaning treatment and language of hip-hop and pop culture. Nanna's questioning of Hustle is McDonald's method of reminding her readers that the state of hip-hop is in jeopardy because many entertainers do not take the time to examine the effects of the images and lyrics in their music and videos. Hip-hop culture is being called into question more often these days. Public forums and town hall meetings are being held across the country regarding the impact that hip-hop culture has on our youth. The tension between art and so-called trash is being debated. At the root of these debates is the concern for whether rap music, for instance, only purports to *do* something as a way of distracting its listeners from actually taking action. It is one thing to assert that hip-hop music has a political impact, but such impact means nothing if there is no tangible evidence of positive change as a result of the music.

In his book, *All About The Beat: Why Hip-Hop Can't Save Black America* (2008), John McWhorter, a leading scholar of hip-hop culture, asserts that, "This [hip-hop] music has less to teach us than we are told. Hip-hop fans ridicule critics of the music as taking the violence and the misogyny too seriously. It's just music they often say—but then at the same time, thrill to people talking about hip-hop as political and revolutionary" (12). It is as if supporters of hip-hop culture want it both ways. McWhorter dismisses the treatment of rap music as being a vehicle for political change. He instead believes that "Hip-hop presents nothing useful to forging political change in the real world. It's all about attitude and just that. It's just music. Good music, but just music" (*All About The Beat*, 12). McWhorter's words and McDonald's beliefs about rap music's influence on our youth are not meant to be negative more than they are meant to be realistic in their eyes. Like McWhorter, McDonald was an avid listener of rap music, which included a list of favorites. However, McDonald did not see rap music as a political force and thus she did not care to create a character whose growing social and political awareness was born solely out of rap lyrics. Instead, Hustle's character was given the gift of rapping as a tool to help readers understand his personal shift in self-respect. In other words, Hustle's rap is all about Hustle and in order to demonstrate how one's identity is constructed through elements of culture and history, McDonald includes mention of significant political and creative figures and events as a necessary force in Hustle's growth.

For instance, McDonald adds a history lesson about the 1960s' spoken-word performer, Gil Scott-Heron, who is considered the founding father of rap and the founder of political rap. By comparing Scott-Heron's socially conscious verse to Hustle's lyrics, McDonald helps readers see the contrast between the type generations of rap. The conflicts among rap artists, executives, parents, and politicians revolve around the tensions between freedom of expression and creative license and social responsibility. What is the power of music and lyrics? How does this particular genre maintain its integrity, while at the same time contributing to the creative form known as hip-hop? How does audience matter in this endeavor? Throughout the novel, McDonald conveys Hustle's evolution through his lyrics. These changes occur in tandem with his life experiences.

No Family, No Schoolin', No Skills . . . Zip

McDonald sets the stage for the possibility of connecting emotionally with a self-made family. Hustle's biological parents abandon him, but this does not stop Hustle from being able to bond with friends and other adults. Hustle's best friend Manly "Ride" Freeman convinces his parents that Hustle would be no trouble as a surrogate family member. The Freemans agree to let Hustle live with them under the condition that he stay out of trouble. Although the Freemans are aware of Hustle's past encounters with the law, they take a chance on him and let him into the family. While Hustle is not a demonstrably expressive person, McDonald makes it clear that he appreciates the Freemans' generosity when, at one point in the novel, Mr. Freeman and Ride attend a father-son event. When Hustle returns home and inquires about their whereabouts, Mrs. Freeman tells him where Mr. Freeman and Ride have gone. Hustle is initially hurt by the fact that he is not included in the father-son event and then quickly shakes off his feelings of disappointment.

At another point in the novel, Hustle is invited to the home of his college-bound girlfriend, Jeannette, to meet her grandmother, Anita Simpson, or Nanna as she is called. Hustle has not had the familial connections of grandparents, so he has no clue how to behave appropriately. When he arrives at Jeannette's apartment, he is greeted by Nanna. Because Nanna appears younger than her actual age, Hustle comments on her good looks, which flatters Nanna and embarrasses Jeannette. As a schoolteacher, Ms. Simpson challenges Hustle to consider his lack of education as a root cause of his unrefined social graces. He does not show Nanna respect by commenting on her appearance. He does not use Standard English. He is a high school dropout. To Nanna, all of these things add up to trouble, in that without some level of education and social awareness, Hustle's future is nonexistent. What is worse is that Hustle is friends with her granddaughter, which makes it doubly important that Hustle recognize his tenuous situation. Like the Freemans, Nanna sees Hustle as a member of her community, and the old adage "It takes a village to raise a child" drives her to invest her knowledge in Hustle by teaching him manners, suggesting that he complete his education, and correcting his speech.

The first shift in Hustle's lyrics occurs after a meeting with his probation officer. Hustle is well aware of the chances of being locked up again. He struggles to stay out of trouble, and he recognizes that one missed appointment with his probation officer or one encounter with police, drugs, guns, or violence will land him in jail. During his visit,

Hustle feels frustration toward his probation officer. On one level, he continues to keep her at arm's length, but on another level, he is bothered by the fact that, although it is her job, she refuses to see the changes that have occurred in him. She asks him the same questions at each visit, and when Hustle tells her of his plans for a music career, she dismisses his dreams and recommends a post office job instead. Upon his arrival home from his visit, Hustle writes:

> Uptown it goes down, fella hittin' red ground for nothin'
> Glock-rockin' awe-shocken' soldiers on the wrong battleground ain't
>   nothin'
> The Five-O's, the P.O.'s, got us all on lockdown we nothin' (*Harlem Hustle* 26).[7]

Hustle's lyrics give readers an indication of some of the causes of hopelessness among urban teens. Authority wreaks havoc on teens' self-esteem in that adults say that they support their dreams, but their actions show otherwise. The inclusion of Hustle's lyrics gives voice to his feelings of self-worth, or lack thereof, but at the same time, his words not only convey his growing self-awareness, but have the potential to validate those same feelings in readers of the novel. McDonald validates the frustrations of adolescents through Hustle's lyrics.

It is not that Ms. Simpson believes that Hustle has nothing to offer. On the contrary, she lends the boy an anthology of notable African American poets. Hustle and Ride are surprised to see poetry from Margaret Walker and Gwendolyn Brooks that speaks to the same concerns as do contemporary rappers. Ms. Simpson's reason for giving Hustle the anthology is twofold. She wants Hustle to recognize famous authors who wrote verse about the same topics as he. At the same time, Ms. Simpson wants to expose him to new ways of expression, so that he understands that profane language is not necessary to tell the story. Hustle's art is validated by poets who came before him, such as Langston Hughes, Claude McKay, and the more contemporary spoken-word artist Saul Williams. McDonald's inclusion of the references to early African American poets is evidence that she understands the tastes and concerns of contemporary adolescents, but at the same time, she wants these same adolescents to understand the power of their words and the indelible mark those words will leave on their audiences long after the a rap artist has recorded a final album.

Hustle is inspired by the poets from the anthology. After reading poems by African American writers, his work changes. From his first rap song to the ones that follow his newfound knowledge about African American poets, Hustle's rhymes become more hopeful as he is inspired by Jeannette and Ms. Simpson to examine possible ways that he can move away from his life of crime and on to a more uplifting career:

> This shorty make me wanna stop
> My hoodlum ways and reach the top
> But movin' gear be all I got
> Don't want to end up shot . . . whoa. (*Harlem Hustle* 155)

By novel's end, Hustle's lyrics evolve even further when he turns his attention to peer pressure and anti-intellectualism especially within African American peer groups:

> Go Black Boy, it's ya birthday
> So give birth to a new day
> Richard Wright talked right, right?
> Did that make him white? Aight
> So stop frontin' and get backin' up off
> The booty-cracken', car-jackin', ill-wackin'
> Way you livin'. (*Harlem Hustle* 181)

In an interview, McDonald explained that her goal in conveying Hustle's growth through his lyrics was not to focus on the songs themselves. Instead, through the competing voices of famous poets, writers, and historical figures, McDonald speaks the language of her intended audience in a way that commands their attention. She explained, "If we want young people to listen to us, we need to learn their language so that we can converse with them. In turn, knowing their language will prepare adults to be better listeners."[8]

These Harlem boys, Nate and Hustle, are multidimensional characters. Nate possesses a passion for schooling and for his home community. He has learned to balance the realities of home and school and comes to appreciate both in different ways. Unlike the characterizations of bookish urban teens who suffer from intraracial antipathy, Hustle is not ashamed of where he came from nor is he embarrassed for wanting to expand his horizons. Hustle defies the stereotypes of the street hood. Underneath his cool veneer, Hustle is a sensitive teen who relishes the embrace of supportive friends. As mentioned earlier, Hustle is one of McDonald's favorite characters in all of her books. She liked that, through Hustle, she could reveal the uncertainties that teens face as they quest for adulthood. McDonald explained that she created Hustle to be the alternative to Nate because readers need to understand that college is not the only ticket to success. Such a message is important for teens because the dominant thinking is that a formal education is the only path to a good life.

Hustle, like many urban teens, wants to become a rapper. McDonald explained that it was her intention to make sure Hustle did not, in fact, become a rap artist. Instead, readers watched him become an artist—a street poet.[9] As mentioned earlier, the more Hustle learned about himself and his history, his lyrics pointed toward uplifting messages about surviving adversity and cultural appreciation. As a result—like Nate—Hustle learns a form of code-switching in that he recognizes the importance of self-presentation in the quest to gain confidence and respect. He no longer needs to write lyrics about shoot-outs and sexual conquests in order to gain power and respect. Like the authors of early urban fiction, McDonald contributes to the need for more books that reflect the experiences of those who rarely get a forum in which to speak, and at the same time, her work informs readers who are unfamiliar with the lives of teens who exist outside of the mainstream.

Notes

1. Angela Neal-Barnett, "Being Black: A New Conceptualization of Acting White," in *Forging Links: African American Children Clinical Developmental Perspectives*, ed. A. M. Neal-Barnett, J. Contreras, and K. Kerns (Westport, CT: Greenwood Publishing Group, 2001).

2. Diana Crane, *Fashion and Its Social Agendas: Class, Gender, and Identity in Clothing* (Chicago: University of Chicago Press, 2000).

3. Micheal Eric Dyson, *Is Bill Cosby Right?: or Has the Black Middle Class Lost Its Mind?* (New York: Civitas Books, 2005).

4. David Pluviose, "Study: 'Acting White' Accusation has Damaging Legacy for Black Students," *Diverse: Issues in Higher Education* 23, no. 4 (April 6, 2006): 8.

5. Janet McDonald, interview by Catherine Ross-Stroud, Paris, France, March 13, 2007.

6. *Booklist* 103, no. 7 (December 1, 2006): 39.

7. Geneva Smitherman, *Word from the Mother: Language and African Americans* (New York: Routledge, 2006), 24.

8. John McWhorter. *All About The Beat: Why Hip-Hop Can't Save Black America* (New York: Gotham Books, 2008).

8. Ross-Stroud interview.

9. Janet McDonald, interview for Farrar, Straus, Giroux, www.fsgkidsbooks.com/audiovideo.htm (accessed). March 20, 2007.

CHAPTER FIVE

~

Shifting Gears: Girls of Color

In 2005, a sixteen-year-old Manhattan teen, Kiri Davis, conducted a research study that would form the basis for her documentary film that chronicles the existence of colorism in contemporary society. As part of the documentary, Davis interviewed five black female adolescents about the issue of race within and outside of the black community. All of the teens in the film concluded that the self-images of black children are hurt by the superimposed images of whiteness that are placed before them in every aspect of their lives. These teens understand the unspoken language of the standards of beauty in our society. To be thin, have straight hair, and have white features are the primary beauty standards for women. Within the black community, the standards include an expectation that females should have light skin and long hair. The teens in Davis's film, *A Girl Like Me*, express feelings of anxiety due to the expectations that are placed upon them, but they also have come to understand that racial ideologies are so embedded in our consciousness that there is no way to combat the situation.

Not only did Davis interview teens, she also reenacted the 1950s' study originally conducted by Kenneth Clark, titled "The Doll Test." In this experiment, small children are presented with two dolls, one white, the other black. The children are then asked to identify the good doll and the bad doll. As in the original study, the black children overwhelmingly chose the white doll as the good doll. These same children were confounded when asked to select the bad doll but consistently chose the black doll—the doll that looked like them. When queried about why they had selected the black doll, the participants could not articulate their reasons, nor could they explain how a doll that resembles them is bad. Davis's purpose for reconducting this older study was to ascertain whether feelings about race and self-concept among black children have changed since *Brown v. Board of Education*, the landmark desegregation law. If we listen to the results of Davis's study, not much has changed. Black children remain confused about their perceptions of blackness and how their self-worth is affected by ideologies of race and racism. It is astounding how much race matters in teens' identity development.

On the issue of race, McDonald had no definite standpoint. In her memoir, McDonald shares her feelings about being called "yellow" by her older sister. The label confused McDonald because, while her skin is lighter than her sister's, she did not consider herself to be light skinned. McDonald's early experience with colorism, where the degree of one's skin color is used as a baseline measurement of one's worth within a particular racial group, set the tone for her struggle with her own identity. What McDonald could not recognize, however, is that perhaps her sister's taunting had something to do with McDonald's status within the family. Of all the McDonald children, Janet was labeled college material by their father. Ann's anger over McDonald's title could not have been easy to live with, and so in order to understand why her sister was so valued by their father, Ann concluded that it must have been Janet's light skin. Ann's behavior is representative of an aspect of colorism referred to as being *color-struck*.

While it might be easy to judge Ann for her unfeeling behavior, it is important to recognize that it was indicative of her experiences growing up as a dark-skinned person. Not only did colorism set the tone for intraracial relations during slavery, more contemporary enactments of color prejudice have taken place on many college campuses across the country. For instance, black fraternities and sororities at historically black universities imposed the paper bag test as a tool for deciding on the admittance of would-be members. If one's skin turned out to be darker than a paper lunch sack, admittance was denied. Spike Lee's

1988 movie, *School Daze*, addresses the deep-seated anxiety that is experienced by both dark-skinned and light-skinned people who have not fully come of age and accepted their identities. *School Daze* is the story of two groups, the Jigaboos and the Wannabees, who are at odds with one another on the basis of skin tone and hair length and texture. The resolution of the film is loosely constructed as neither group works through their various anxieties. Instead, the Wannabees are uncovered as being phony and the Jigaboos are concluded to have low self-esteem due to having African features. These dichotomous readings of race leave no room for negotiating worth based on other attributes. One belongs on one side or the other, and although the descriptors for each category are not articulated, these elements are identified in our everyday lives.

In fiction as well adolescent characters confront issues of colorism head-on. In Jacqueline Woodson's *The House You Pass on the Way* (1997), Staggerlee Canan is confronted with the social isolation that is a result of her biracial heritage. Her mother is white and thus part of Staggerlee's struggle to fit into the mostly black community. At one point in Maya Angelou's 1969 autobiography *I Know Why the Caged Bird Sings*, Maya wishes for white skin because she believes life in the Deep South would be easier for her if she were not black. Although Maya does not face criticism about her skin tone from the black community, she assumes that her grandmother's polite treatment of racist white people is due to their whiteness, not the politics of the South that would make retaliation against whites from blacks punishable by death. In each of these books, the characters face colorism and that encounter changes the way they feel about themselves. Moreover, Maya Angelou and the fictional Staggerlee are representative of actual teens who struggle to find a positive racial designation for themselves. The more instances of color prejudice black adolescents face, the more unstable their sense of self becomes.

McDonald's conflict with her racial identity is exacerbated when her sister's "yellow" moniker becomes more ruthless. The further McDonald excelled in school, the more rewards were bestowed upon her by her parents, and the more anger developed in Ann. By the time McDonald was accepted to the academically rigorous Erasmus Hall Academy, Ann had graduated from her labeling to prophesizing that Janet would one day turn into a white girl. Ann's words frightened McDonald because if she did, in fact, turn white, she would no longer belong as a member of her family and her community. McDonald's experience with an aspect of colorism set the tone for how she felt about herself throughout her teens and early adulthood. Thus, it is important to consider the impact of race and also of the politics of colorism within the black community in order to be able to understand just how complicated growing up black in America can be.

The term *color-struck* is one that ignites tension in the black community. The notion of being color-struck dates back to slavery, when mulatto slaves were afforded privileges by virtue of their fair skin tone. Black children get their education in colorism early. The little black girl whose mother has to struggle to untangle tightly curled hair will desire that her children have "good hair" or hair with a fine texture, devoid of the wooly feel and tightly wound curls. Like Pecola Breedlove in Toni Morrison's 1970 novel *The Bluest Eye*, these children recognize that knowing smile of teachers and other adults when a light-skinned child is in their presence. Growing up black is a struggle for some children, and often the challenges they face have to do with their skin tone. While adults admire the European features of a fair-skinned child, dark-skinned children often have other ideas. While teachers smiled on Maureen Peel in *The Bluest Eye*, black children called her names such as "dogtooth meringue pie" in order to assuage their feelings of hurt and resentment due to the rejection they experienced on a daily basis. If the issue of colorism presents challenges in the lives of black children, imagine what life would be like after the discovery that the white identity one has become accustomed to is erased.

Who is the Fairest of Them All?

Like most of McDonald's writing, her short story "Zebra Girl" contains characters that share similarities with the people in her life. In "Zebra Girl," sisters Nadine and Dale Lutter share a close relationship that later turns bitter. Sixteen-year-old Nadine is dark skinned with long silky hair. Twelve-year-old Dale is fair skinned with short curly hair. The girls' friendship flourishes until Dale begins school. As a kindergartner, Dale gets exposed to color politics by a teacher who comments on her light skin and calls her beautiful. Dale internalizes the teacher's remarks and equates beauty with light skin. The teacher said, "I (Dale) am the pretty one and Nadine would be pretty too if she had light skin."[1] But it is Nadine who is the most affected by Dale's confession. Nadine is confronted with color politics again, when, in the sixth grade, another teacher comments on her skin color. Mr. Hill takes attendance, recognizes Nadine's last name and asks if she is related to Dale "the pretty second grader?" When Nadine tells him she is Dale Lutter's sister, Mr. Hill says, "Amazing. You two look nothing at all alike." Mr. Hill's words damage the sisters' friendship even further. Nadine declares that she hates Mr. Hill, and she also begins to antagonize Dale by calling her zebra girl. Nadine and Dale's relationship is similar to that of McDonald and her sister Ann. Just as Ann resented Janet's reputation as college material, Nadine felt short-changed by the attention that Dale's light skin garnered. And just as Ann torments Janet with name-calling, so does Nadine. Angered by her feelings of devaluation, Nadine searches for a way to make Dale suffer. The contrast between the dark and the light skin on Dale's feet reminds Nadine of a zebra's coat, and so she comes up with the nickname that would be used to torment Dale: "Zebra Girl."

While colorism affects everybody, special attention should be paid to why women of color are especially devastated. According to Margaret Hunter in her book, *Race, Gender, and the Politics of Skin Tone*, we must take into consideration the history of colorism as it relates to gender. She asserts that "Notions of beauty are so closely related to color that the terms 'light-skinned' and 'pretty' were nearly synonymous."[2] Hunter's research findings confirm the fact that there is "An intense concern about light skin color as a status characteristic. Light skin was seen as a device for approval in families, as well as a near prerequisite for the designation of 'beautiful.' It was the focal point of jealousies between female friends and family members."[3] Ann's and Nadine's reactions to colorism are realistic portrayals of the struggles that dark-skinned girls face because they implicitly understand that their femininity is related to their beauty and their beauty is tied to their skin color. While there are privileges to having light skin—more date and marriage prospects, career advancement based on the conflation of light skin with beauty and intelligence, and acceptance into wider social settings[4]—Hunter reminds us that there are also disadvantages to having light skin: "resentment and distrust from darker-skinned women, and possibly fewer opportunities for female friendship."[5] Nadine and Dale mend their relationship fairly quickly; however, it was a long time before McDonald was able to come to terms with the tension between herself and Ann. "Zebra Girl" conveys McDonald's understanding of how colorism can negatively influence people of color's lives both at home and in the larger society. The roots of color consciousness are deep. As mentioned earlier, the privileging of light-skinned black people during slavery continues into contemporary society. The often-hidden phenomenon of intraracial antipathy in minority communities has become the subject of research and television documentaries. In 2005, the ABC news program *20/20* aired an episode titled "Skin Deep Discrimination: Colorism Shows We're a Long Way from a Color-Blind Society." John Stossel conducted a survey where he provided sixty color-distorted images of people from various racial categories. He asked his respondents to rate each person in the pictures in terms of their beauty, wealth, and intelligence. He found that both African Americans and white Americans rated the light-skinned images higher than the darker images. Stossel concluded that while there is talk of a colorblind society, our core beliefs about race suggest that color prejudice has not ended. In a 2006 study of dating preferences of black college students, Ashraf Esmail found that while light-skinned blacks have an advantage in the realm of dating opportunities, the respondents in the study asserted that when it comes to selecting a marriage partner, the skin tone of their opposite-sexed parent is often comparable to that of their selected partner.[6] Overall, however, the preference for lighter skin remains a constant concern in the black community.

Off-Color

McDonald's concern for how adolescents in general and black teens in particular view themselves in terms of race is further explored in *Off-Color*. McDonald said that *Off-Color* was the book that held the most meaning for her. It is the only book of hers that has, as readers are initially led to believe, a white protagonist who ends up moving to the projects. A white project girl? McDonald says that *Off-Color* is special to her in personal ways. First, *Off-Color* was written in its entirety while she battled her illness. Second, since the idea to create a white project girl was given to her by her agent, McDonald had to struggle with how she, a black writer, would be able to write about a white character. The process of producing a quality text that does not rely on commonplace narratives or mere reversal of racial stereotypes meant that McDonald had to take her agent's suggestion and then construct a character who is plausible and unique at the same time. McDonald explained that "she had planned to write about characters of many races, but she wanted the novels to be different and stereotype free."[7] *Off-Color*, in McDonald's estimation, fits that standard.

A Question of Race
Cameron's life is ordinary, filled with teen angst, school, friends, and the quest for autonomy. *Off-Color* offers readers the pressing issue of coming of age: the quest for an authentic identity. McDonald explained that the protagonist of *Off-Color*, Cameron, is modeled after one of her relatives. At a family reunion she attended while in her teens, she and her other cousins noticed a white girl milling around family, and, judging by the way she was treated by the adults, it was evident that this white girl was a family member. McDonald explained that she was perplexed by the fact that this girl had pale skin, blue eyes, and blonde hair. There was that faint recognition of "black" features that is often described when the subject of racial passing is brought up. However, those markers, such as the width of the nose, shape of the lips, and a lilt in the voice are not always reliable when attempting to categorize race. Having gotten over the shock that this girl, in fact, was a relative, McDonald began to wonder about her own racial identity, in that she questioned whether or not we have the right to categorize and define other people.

While McDonald was a student at Columbia University's journalism school, she met another woman with the same features as the cousin from her past. For reasons unknown to her then, the memories of these two women stayed with McDonald and ultimately surfaced as Cameron Storm's narrative in *Off-Color*. McDonald's historical knowledge regarding racial passing and its consequences became the frame on which McDonald constructed the plot of the novel. Historically, when one passed for white and was found out, there were extreme penalties, including the possibility of being lynched. The parallel, then, was drawn in this book, but with a contemporary questioning of the consequences of being found out as racially passing. The decision to create a character who is completely unaware of her racial status had more to do with the goal to avoid creating a character who suffers from racial self-hatred. It is important, according to McDonald, that her characters exude a sense of "black love" instead of self-hatred.[8]

Othello and All Things Ambiguous

Unlike *Brother Hood* and *Harlem Hustle*, *Off-Color* is not dense with references to literary classics, historical facts, and monuments. Instead, Cameron's narrative includes only a few references to items of cultural literacy. The novel opens with Cameron preparing for school among the ubiquitous shouts and warnings of tardiness from a parent. Cameron's arrival is met with the normal issues—a counselor speaks to her about her grades and her attendance record because she has been skipping classes. Cameron's school is integrated, but not heavily, and at this point in the novel, Cameron is identified as white and all of her friends are white. Race does not become a topic of conversation until well into the novel, when Cameron's English class is reading Shakespeare's *Othello*. The students begin class by complaining that they do not understand the play, with its odd language style and alleged misspelling of words. Mr. Robinson, the teacher, interjects a challenge into the students' ranting: "Think O. J. Simpson" (*Off-Color* 31). This sets off a series of statements from the students regarding the Simpson case and O. J. and the question of his guilt or innocence. The parallel that McDonald sets up in the novel is an effective literary device used to help both readers and the students in Mr. Robinson's classroom understand the timelessness of literary classics. The students' initial experience with *Othello* is one of alienation; however, the connection between past and present reinforces McDonald's assertion that the classics matter and that setting a context for reading will inspire adolescent readers to delve into the past in order to find relevance in the present.

At the same time, however, McDonald's strategy of including the *Othello* discussion foreshadows Cameron's impending identity crisis. One student says, "It [*Othello*] is about being different" (*Off-Color* 32). Cameron's assessment of the play is poignant:

> It seemed like they all had race issues. I felt sorry for Othello because he was all tripped out about being a Moor, you know, black, and that's how Iago was able to make him believe his wife was cheating on him with a white guy. (*Off-Color* 32)

Cameron's comments regarding the play are extra-diegetic in that, through Cameron, readers are reminded of what W. E. B. Du Bois asserted in 1903: "The problem of the twentieth century is the problem of the color line."[9] McDonald's strategy of using recursive narration demonstrates that race was a problem in the seventeenth century and is a pressing concern in the millennium. For instance, McDonald includes a scene where, still unaware of her blackness, Cameron and her friends have an encounter with a group of black girls. Cameron and her friends label the black girls as "project Grrrls because of their two-inch-polka-dot fingernails, fake ponytails, skin tight jeans and mid-drift shirts" (*Off-Color* 42). One of the white girls comments that being from the projects is nothing to be proud of because it "means you are poor, black, on welfare, and wear booty clothes" (*Off-Color* 42). The encounter gets more complicated when the black girls hear Cameron and her friends make fun of them by using Black English Vernacular mixed with slang, while gesturing with their bodies in order to mimic what they perceive to be the project communication style. The project girls accuse Cameron's group of mocking black people, which leads to a near-physical confrontation. This scene is just one of many in McDonald's work that convey the ever-present racial tension that still exists in the twenty-first century.

Categorizing Urban Youth

Furthermore, the confrontation between the project girls and Cameron's friends also addresses issues of social class. In this sense, readers get a sense of the ideological positioning of race and class and how these elements are often conflated. The assumption that the project girls are actually from public housing is made by the white girls' visual assessment of the group. We categorize teen culture and fashion in terms of race and class. Midriff tops and fancy fingernails are often attributed to black females. Project girls are often referred to as ghetto girls because it is assumed that this particular style of dress is worn only by poor black girls. Popular culture often portrays the project girl as loud, physically well-developed, and extreme in affect. "Ghetto fabulous" is the term most often used to describe a project girl's lifestyle and station in life. Ghetto fabulous is a term bound up in class issues. Popular culture portrays ghetto fabulous aesthetic as evoked by those who grow up poor and then somehow, either through luck, fame, or hard work, gain disposable income, which they spend on nonnecessities. These items are often ostentatious, verging on tacky. Thus, large gold chains, even larger hoop earrings, and cheap clothing are considered the aesthetic of the ghetto chic. Diane Crane (2000) explains that the move toward an "outsider" manner of appearance is related issues of power.[10] Historically, "Clothing was useful for 'blurring' social standing, as a means of breaking away from social constraints, and of appearing to have more social or economic resources than was actually the case" (Crane, 67). And this breaking away from constraints is most often enacted by those who suffer perceived or real consequences of belonging to an oppressed group. Thus, if one feels powerless in just about every aspect of their lives, then physical appearance can be the way to claim a level of control over one's identity. Clothing and fashion as a means of self-expression are not a new concept; however, in the case of the ghetto couture aesthetic, the goal is to infuse a nonconventional outlaw affect with just a hint of traditional dress.

Moreover, material goods alone do not make up the entire aesthetic. There is an affect of pride when the ghetto fabulous person has an audience. Thus, the girls in the hamburger shop become loud and exaggerate their speech and body language when they recognize that there are onlookers (Cameron and her friends) for whom to perform. Much of the fuel that drives the ghetto fabulous stereotype has to do with how the public reacts to people who are perceived as belonging to the category. It is socially acceptable to parody ghetto fabulousness and these parodies can be performed by people from many different races. Sometimes even men portray the ghetto fabulous women by costuming themselves in female clothing and then performing the ghetto girl behavior. In this instance, the performance is usually meant to be comedic.

In certain circumstances, the ghetto fabulous persona moves from comic relief to fear. For instance, in *Spellbound*, Aisha's reaction to the receptionist who is rude to Raven makes the woman fearful, and so she becomes more forthright with the information that Raven is requesting. In *Brother Hood*, Nate changes from being a well-dressed prep school student, which instills no fear in the train passengers, into his project clothes in Grand Central Station. The result is that pass-ersby in the station veer away from him as they pass, and others place a stronger hold on their purses. Thus the ghetto fabulous persona of the male is also viewed as predatory. Urban teens are often placed in nega-tive categories. The urban teen affect is often seen as rebellion against authority and the status quo. In the case of Cameron and her friends, these project girls represent a disturbance to their world and so they should be made fun of or feared.

The New Project Girl
With Cameron and her friends' definition of a project girl in their heads, it is no secret that becoming a project girl themselves would be devastating. Unfortunately, Cameron must confront this very fear. Cameron is an only child who lives with her single mother. She does not have any knowledge about her biological father; she assumes he is missing or dead. Ms. Storm's single-parent status and lack of formal education means that she must take low-paying jobs. The result is that the Storms live in a one-bedroom apartment where Cameron sleeps in the bedroom and her mother sleeps on the sofa. The housing arrange-ment works well for Cameron and her mother because they get to live in a safe area of Brooklyn with good schools. The trade-off for these luxuries is that Ms. Storm cannot afford a larger place for them to live; however, all is well until Cameron's mother loses her job.

When the beauty salon where Ms. Storm works shuts down, it leaves her vulnerable to eviction from her apartment and unable to pay her bills. Luckily, Ms. Storm's boss, Ms. Elga, has an opening in one of her stores across town in a black neighborhood. Patricia reluctantly accepts the position with the understanding that the salary for that position is lower because the clientele is different, so the prices for services are less. In order to survive on a lower salary, Patricia needs to move to a cheaper apartment. When Ms. Elga suggests that she get her name on the list for the projects located near the salon where she works, Patricia initially rejects the idea but later accepts that she has no choice but to move to the projects.

The news of the move devastates Cameron. Like her friends, she has preconceived notions about the environment in the projects. McDonald is careful to provide evidence for comparison of perceptions versus realities in Cameron's dilemma. She has spent so much time judging those unlike her, and now she has become one of *them*. Now she must negotiate her relationship with her friends, who share her beliefs about project girls. She wonders if they will remain her friends, and she is frightened by the possibility of switching schools. Cameron's comfort level is nonexistent at this point.

Colorism: Discovering the Self through Pictures

McDonald's awareness of identity and the politics of skin color is re-vealed throughout the novel. The most often-used explanation for the colorism phenomenon dates back to slavery, when mulatto slaves were valued more than African slaves, and so they were given house posi-tions while their darker counterparts toiled in the sizzling heat. The dichotomous positioning of dark and light meant that mulatto slaves were left with no community at all. In *Off-Color*, McDonald examines the issue of colorism from a historical point of view and then from a contemporary standpoint when Cameron and her friends debate about the race of popular celebrities. Is Mariah Carey black? Do white celebri-ties who want to be cool adopt the behaviors that are considered black, such as a swagger in the walk and truncated speech? In the search for identity, issues of race weigh heavily on the thoughts, feelings, and actions of adolescents. As a result, while there is discourse that asserts that color no longer matters, McDonald reminds us that teens are savvy enough to recognize early on that color does matter.

Cameron's discovering the truth of her race is devastating. However, while she is disturbed because her mother lies to her about having a father, her confusion regarding her identity is the most pressing issue for her. Upon reflection, she acknowledges some of the clues that were always present about her race: the thick lips, the tightly curled hair, the fact that she tanned darker than her white friends, African Americans who tell her that she looks like one of their relatives. While it can be argued that Cameron is aware of her racial makeup all along, perhaps the larger issue in this text has to do with the construction of social identity rather than racial identity. Cameron's character, then, gives voice to the question, "Who am I and who gets to define me?" In her book *Why Are All the Black Kids Sitting Together in the Cafeteria?* Beverly Daniel Tatum sheds light on these questions regarding adolescence and racial identity. Tatum surmises that the tendency toward racial categorization means that children get messages about which group they belong to in early childhood. In the case of biracial children such as Cameron, however, the designation is more complicated. Most often, a child's racial designation correlates with the "one drop" rule where if the child is multiracial, they land in the category of the minority race. Thus, Cameron would be black. On the other hand, if the parents of a biracial child are no longer living together, then the child's racial identity is deemed that of the custodial parent. Both situations are further complicated by the fact that outward appearance sometimes conflicts with racial designation, which takes identity confusion to another dimension. As a result, according to Tatum, biracial adolescents face the task of having to "sort through the various factors and find a way to integrate them into a positive sense of self."[11]

Unfortunately for Cameron, however, she does not have a positive view of black people. Like many individuals who do not have direct and daily contact with black people, she gets her information about their racial and cultural characteristics from mediated sources. Cameron has multiple tasks ahead of her. First, she needs to become acquainted with the black side of her identity. Second, she has to endure the potential fallout in terms of her social status among her friends. Having moved to the projects shifts Cameron's social status. Add a change in racial identity, and the potential for loss of social status among her peers increases.

The construction of Cameron's character is consistent with the traits of protagonists in McDonald's other novels: Cameron is smart, strong, and sensible. As a result, the novel does not resort to the tendency of some stories with similar plots such as Kate Chopin's *Desiree's*

Baby (1893), Fannie Hurst's *Imitations of Life* (1933), and Toni Morrison's *The Bluest Eye*, where the question of race foreshadows a tragic ending for the protagonist. Instead, McDonald remains loyal to her commitment to create characters who can handle whatever challenges face them. McDonald explains: "What is important for my readers to recognize is that while the characters in my books do not have charmed lives, they take on whatever challenge that is given to them and in the end, they are okay."[12]

Cameron moves past her devastation in order to find support for handling her situation. She finds solidarity with Mr. Siciliano, her guidance counselor, who reveals that he is aware of her racial identity. Perplexed, Cameron questions his knowledge. He explains that he is biracial as well. Unlike Cameron, however, Mr. Siciliano did not have the luxury of choosing a "side." His mother is black and his father is Italian American. His skin is too dark to pass for white and too light to be accepted into the black peer group in the housing project where he grew up. Mr. Siciliano chose to instead identity himself as Puerto Rican in order to wrestle himself out of the social conflicts that come with biracial identity politics.

Cameron does Internet research in order to find information about multiracial people. She finds that celebrities such as Barack Obama, Count Basie, and Vin Diesel are of biracial descent. This information is comforting to Cameron, while at the same time, the information helps her revise her assumptions about nonwhite people to the point where "she felt a burst of new self emerging, one that was richer, rounded, colorful" (*Off-Color* 110). Cameron accepts that she will struggle with racial concerns, and she accepts her identity and thus is able to feel more comfortable with herself. Although her old friends stay in touch with her, Cameron needs to connect with black teens as well. The decision to change from her mostly white school to a more integrated school signals Cameron's developing self-acceptance. Racial adjustment is not the only task that Cameron will have to tackle. Cameron's relocation to the projects makes it necessary for her to revise her definition of identity based on location. Cameron's quest is social in nature as she will not only have to fight the stereotypes of race and gender, she will also be charged with the duty of fighting perceptions of the ghetto girl stereotype. In order to do so, Cameron must first reflect on her own beliefs to discover the origins of the assumptions she has made about black people who live in the projects. These tasks are monumental for Cameron because as an adolescent female, she already struggles with body image in terms of the physical and emotional changes that occur as a result of her age. How will Cameron redirect the perceptions of herself from concerns of white female adolescents with body image and social status to black female adolescents' understanding of body image and social status?

In her biotheoretical work titled *Notes of a White Black Woman: Race, Color, Community*, Judy Scales-Trent explores her own experiences of coming of age as a black female who appears physically to be white. Scales-Trent interrogates the definitions of race in order to decide for herself what we mean when we use the term *race* in our society. Her simultaneous existence both within and outside of the black community gives her insight into how racial categories are defined based both on skin tone and social positioning. Scales-Trent underpins her explanation of racial categorization by calling upon the quest to maintain racial purity in the United States. Racial purity is both practiced and theorized in that the first step in deciding who belongs and who does not begins with skin tone. Thus, a white family that moves into a predominantly white neighborhood would call no attention to itself. However, if the white family suffered particular class failings that mark them as lower in economic and social class than the remaining residents, then their racial status is called into question, as being low on the class register is equated with categories other than whiteness. If that same family was comprised of fair-skinned blacks who could pass as white, then that family would initially be assumed to be white by virtue of the proximity rule that states that since this family resides within a similar class structure, and their skin is white, then they are white—especially if there are no class failings being committed. A visibly black family, then, registers differently to those who use skin tone as the indicator of race. They are measured based on their social and class standing, in which expectations of at least middle-class and preferably upper-class status in work and family are applied.

Cameron's move from a middle-class or working-class integrated neighborhood to the projects immediately sets into action the process of giving up the privilege of being given the benefit of the doubt in particular areas of her life. Where project girls are read as poor and un-educated, white girls who do not live in the projects are, until proven to be otherwise, not categorized in the same way. As a result, Cameron will have to continually revise these stereotypical narratives on two levels: first, if it is taken for granted that she is white Cameron might want to enlighten others that she is black. If she is categorized as poor and thus written off as unworthy of recognition, she will have had the experience of being both the one who dismisses and the one who is dis-missed. In such a situation, her experiences will provide an opportunity for her to initiate change within both of her peer groups, in that her knowledge will be based on experience. On the other hand, Cameron will face the pressure of finding a category for herself based on race. The tendency to categorize multiracial people based on the facets of their identity relating to race creates a situation where multiracial people are forced to choose a "side," which leads to the diminishing importance of the complexity of their identity and culture. Cameron's decision to transfer to a predominantly black school and to create bonds with the black girls in her housing project has the potential of negating some of the aspects of her white identity in much the same way.

The attitudes and behaviors of her mother add to the danger of Cam-eron's potential for negating her black identity. As mentioned earlier, Cameron did not have a high opinion of black people. Ms. Storm was concealing the fact that Cameron's father is black. Cameron's formative years were not informed by positive representations of blackness. The discovery of her father's racial identity and the move to the projects have the power to change her beliefs if her mother provides positive feedback regarding blackness. It will not be enough for Ms. Storm to continue to ignore racial issues altogether as she has done in the past. Instead, she will need to come to terms with the abandonment she suf-fered from Cameron's father and its potential to be connected to racial stereotypes of black male irresponsibility in family commitments.

By the novel's end, Cameron begins to reestablish her racial identity. William Poston's Biracial Identity Development model (1990) helps to explain Cameron's journey.[13] It consists of five stages: personal identity, choice of group categorization, enmeshment/denial, appreciation, and integration. As mentioned earlier, race was not a crucial concern dur-ing Cameron's formative years. Cameron's physical appearance and her

mother's whiteness equaled whiteness. Thus, Cameron's struggles centered mostly around her developing sense of self in the typical woes of a
teenager: academic apathy, depression, and peer acceptance. The move
to the projects and the discovery of her biracial identity precipitates the
second stage of Cameron's resocialization. Although she is devastated
by the discovery of her black father, Cameron is more concerned with
her peer group standing and whether or not she will lose her friends.
Denial/enmeshment, the third stage of Poston's model, occurs when
Cameron tries to hide the fact that she is biracial, but at the same time,
she explores what it means to have black roots. The conversation with
her biracial guidance counselor and the subsequent Internet research
that Cameron conducts help her feelings of anger and denial subside.
The fourth stage of Cameron's journey occurs when she gets to know
some of the black girls in her neighborhood and reveals to her classmates that she is biracial. While Cameron suffers a lot of discomfort at
this stage, she no longer feels the pressure to hide her feelings of guilt
and doubt regarding her previous assumptions about what it means to
be black. Stage five, the integration stage of Poston's model, entails
an acceptance of self and a level of celebration for the diverse aspects
of one's multiracial identity. The novel ends with Cameron attending
an African World Music concert. It is telling that McDonald locates
Cameron's identity resolution within the context of her blackness.

A character such as Cameron is plausible in that so many biracial
people never learn their true racial background and those who do
learn about their heritage often do not find out until they are older.
McDonald's neatly packed ending of *Off-Color*, however, is idealistic
in that due to the complexities of racial discord in society, simply
accepting one's racial difference and making the journey toward resocialization is not so easy.

Notes

1. Janet McDonald, "Zebra Girl," in *Skin Deep*, ed. Tony Bradman (London:
Puffin, 2004), 5.

2. Margaret Hunter, *Race, Gender, and the Politics of Skin Tone* (New York:
Routledge, 2005), 70.

3. Hunter, *Race, Gender, and the Politics of Skin Tone*, 70.

4. See Obiagele Lake, *Blue Veins and Kinky Hair: Naming and Color Consciousness in African America* (Westport, CT: Praeger, 2003).

5. Hunter, *Race, Gender, and the Politics of Skin Tone*, 89.

6. Ashraf Esmail and Jas Sullivan, "African American College Males and Females: A Look at Color Mating Preferences," *Race, Class, Gender* 13 (1) (2006): 201–20.

7. Janet McDonald, interview by Catherine Ross-Stroud, Paris, March 13, 2007.

8. Ross-Stroud interview.

9. W. E. B. Du Bois, *The Souls of Black Folk* (New York: Vintage, 1990).

10. Diane Crane, *Fashion and Its Social Agenda: Class, Gender, and Identity in Clothing* (Chicago: University of Chicago Press, 2000).

11. Beverly D. Tatum, *Why Are All the Black Kids Sitting Together in the Cafeteria? And Other Conversations about Race* (New York: Basic Books, 1997), 185.

12. Ross-Stroud interview.

13. W. S. C. Poston, "The Biracial Identity Development Model: A Needed Addition," *Journal of Counseling and Development* (69) (1990): 152–55.

CHAPTER SIX

~

Urban Fiction: Answering the Call

Janet McDonald's goal for writing books not exclusively for, but mainly about, black teens was to give voice to the lesser-known experiences of coming of age as an African American. She writes:

> My books house teen mothers, high school dropouts, shoplifting home-boys, preppy drug dealers, and girl arsonists. A few characters are gay, others are straight. Most strive to achieve a positive goal; some seek little more than their idle, pointless status quo. But it is not only the down and nearly out who are represented. The cast also includes paralegals, college kids, teenage entrepreneurs, computer-savvy project girls, and budding artists.[1]

McDonald's mission answers the call of such writers as Toni Morrison, who asserts that "it was her desire to write about the people in literature who were always peripheral—little black girls who were props, back-ground."[2] Similarly, prolific young adult novelist Walter Dean Myers asserts that his reasons for writing books for a black teen audience are born out of his quest to "provide for black children good literature," which he defines as "literature that includes them and the way they live" and that "celebrates their life and their person. It upholds and gives special place to their humanity."[3] These calls for more literature that presents the black adolescent experience in realistic terms still rage on today. However, McDonald wanted to stretch the body of literature to include themes and characters that made it their goal to step beyond their reality in order to expand their concept of self. McDonald explains that her characters are similar and also different from black characters in the work of black urban teen novelists such as Myers, and the differences most often have to do with the autobiographical connection that her novels have to her own life.

Urban Literature: Background

The status of urban fiction as a literary genre is enmeshed in lively debate. Urban fiction is a body of literature that reflects the lived experiences, cultural protocols, and language traditions of urban, particularly black, people.[4] Like certain forms of rap music, urban fiction is often labeled a bad influence on adolescent readers, because such texts are extremely graphic and often portray characters that are considered by those outside of the intended reading audience to be unworthy of emulation. However, just as hardcore rap music gives a voice to those who feel alienated from the discourse of power, readers of urban literature affirm the struggles of urban existence that are often ignored by the larger society. Much of the literature that urban teens encounter does not represent their realities. Instead, these books often communicate the traditions and values of the white middle class. While it is not safe to say that all urban teens fail to see the value of mainstream literature, it is safe to say that these teens want to see their lives portrayed in what they read. Adolescent readers in general desire literature that speaks to them and speaks to their experiences, and the same is true in terms of the representation of culture in the books they read.[5]

That said, proponents of urban fiction find themselves constantly on the defensive in terms of questions regarding the literary quality of these books. Traditional African American literature was born out of the uplift tradition where the major requirement for black literature was that it represented the best of blackness. Thus, writers such as Zora Neale Hurston were often challenged because her stories challenged bourgeois notions of blackness. Hurston's characters speak in Black English Vernacular. They are working class and sometimes poverty stricken, often farmers, and they sometimes represent the oppressive elements of gender and race. The leaders of the uplift tradition, W. E. B. Du Bois and Alaine Locke, called for black artists to be aware of the negative stereotypes of blackness in order for their work to act as a mechanism to reverse those beliefs. Thus, representations of language, family, class, and race are bound up in the quest to change the minds of white people who believed black people to be the antithesis of civility. The call for uplifting art and writing was made by black scholars in the early twentieth century, and in certain circles is still an unspoken imperative today. As a result, works that highlight explicit sexuality, drugs, crime, and poverty go against the quest to improve the image of blacks in the eyes of those who hold a negative view of the race.

Supporters of urban fiction assert that their work represents a previously silenced sector of the black population. These writers believe that their writing promotes literacy in the black community. Vicki Stringer's Triple Crown Publishing Company, for instance, based in Columbus, Ohio, has published numerous hip-hop titles, of which over one million paperback copies have been sold. The readership of urban fiction is mostly women ranging from ages fifteen to twenty-five. The male readership is growing as well. These readers had not previously frequented bookstores and libraries in the search for reading material, and it is estimated that these novels produce income for independent bookstores that ranges in the millions of dollars. Urban fiction authors believe that their work has a lot to offer young readers in terms of navigating an urban existence. For instance, Noire, a prominent hip-hop author, explains, "All my books are cautionary street tales and my characters get dragged real low through the mud because of the bad decisions they make in life. I show people exactly what happens when they choose that fast, get-money, grimy life, and that's what real street fiction is all about."[6] In this sense, urban fiction can be said to serve a purpose for an audience whose life dilemmas are not portrayed in any other venue.

Hip-hop authors also assert that the main reason for traditional black novelists' disdain for their work has more to do with the issue of readership than with overall quality of the literature. While critics such as Nick Chiles call urban fiction smut, the readership for these novels continues to grow. But traditional black novelists object to their work being placed in the same category as urban fiction. For instance, many bookstores place all black authors' work together in the black studies or the African American section of their stores. Major authors and literary critics worry that such a placement does much to dilute the perceived quality of black literature, in that the so-called serious black literature will be confused with the work of hip-hop authors. Moreover, award-winning authors such as Toni Morrison and Gwendolyn Brooks, who are included in most scholarly discussions about great literature, earned this designation by virtue of their standards in scholarship. On the other hand, urban fiction authors are not as careful with editing, storylines, and character development. Hip-hop authors do not purport to be primarily concerned with technical aspects of their work. Instead, these authors prefer to communicate a particular message to a particular group of people. Joylynn Jossel, of Triple Crown Publishing, responds to the criticism regarding the literary quality of the genre. She maintains, "We know that there are many things we can do better, and we're working on it. We want to continue to get better, because we're not just writing books. We're not just trying to make money. We're delivering a message—a point of hope."[7] The need for literature for and about black young adults is nothing new. Prior to the moment when hip-hop literature officially burst onto the scene via publishing houses such as Triple Crown Press, there was the late Donald Goines' work about ghetto life and the struggles of black young adults. All of Goines' young adult characters turned to a life of crime or drugs in order to survive. Despite the fact that Goines' work presented the grime and grit of urban life, he remains the best-selling urban fiction author. In the end, like the battle between supporters and opponents of hip-hop literature, the debate is the same within the realm of adolescent literature.

Early Urban Fiction for Young Adults

Urban fiction for young adults replicates many of the negative images of black people, and as a result, the inclusion of such books in mainstream classrooms is often challenged. Despite the work of censors to silence the voices of urban youth, however, these novels continue to be popular among black teens. Early authors such as Louise Meriwether and Alice Childress provided some of the first insights into urban black teen life. Meriwether's *Daddy Was a Number Runner* (1970), for instance, is set in 1930s' Harlem where the Great Depression wreaked havoc on the lives of its inhabitants. The protagonist of the novel, Francie, endures the hardships that come with urban poverty. Her father is unable to find legal work and as a result he runs numbers for local residents. Francie's mother works as a domestic to help support the family. Francie and her friends are left to navigate the mean streets of Harlem, where pimps, prostitutes, and drug dealers are pervasive. Not only does Francie concern herself with basic survival, she contends with her developing body and the emotions that come with puberty. When Francie gets her period, she is confused as to what is happening to her body, and she is doubly confused about why men begin to look at her differently. Francie is not portrayed as a victim of her circumstances. Instead, Meriwether's careful plot development helps readers to witness how Francie copes with her particular reality without compromising herself in the process.

Childress's *A Hero Ain't Nothin' but a Sandwich* (1973) is the story of Benji, a black teen from a two-parent home who succumbs to drug addiction. Even though Benji lives in an impoverished area, he has more family support than many of his peers and so it is no wonder that his parents, friends, and teachers are distressed by his choice to use drugs. Childress, like Meriwether, is careful not to present readers with an image of downtrodden blackness. Instead, *Hero* helps readers understand that, while one might have all of the support in the world, none of it matters if one chooses to make the wrong decisions. Later authors, such as Walter Dean Myers, focus mainly on black male protagonists from Harlem. His 1988 novel, *Scorpions*, tells the story of twelve-year-old Jamal Hicks. Once Jamal's gang leader brother Randy gets sent to jail for murder, the Scorpions, a local gang, make Jamal their leader. Jamal is reluctant to join, let alone lead a gang; however, he does not want to let his older brother down. Jamal becomes enthralled with a gun that was given to him by one of the gang members and thus participates in the Scorpions' activities, but only peripherally. Jamal wants nothing to do with gangs, and he does not want to end up in jail like his older brother. While the major storyline of *Scorpions* has to do with gang violence in Harlem, Jamal's daily existence is where readers are able to bond with the text. *Scorpions* takes on subjects such as black male alienation from schools and schooling. Jamal is harassed by his school's principal, who wants nothing more than for Jamal to drop out of school completely. He tells Jamal that he will amount to nothing and that he lacks intelligence. Jamal also confronts family conflict. Since Jamal's father abandoned the family, first Randy and then Jamal are left to be the man of things. Jamal resents Randy for being sent to jail because Mrs. Hicks has to rely on her younger son to take care of the house. Jamal also shows anger toward his father, who occasionally visits Mrs. Hicks, usually for a hot meal and a bit of affection. Jamal witnesses the pain that his mother endures when, once he has gotten what he came for, Mr. Hicks abandons her once again. Finally, Myers portrays the importance of friendship between boys. Jamal and his best friend, Tito, support each other emotionally, and then at a pivotal moment in the novel, physically. Thus, while Myers' work, like that of Meriwether and Childress, does not romanticize the realities of urban life, these authors are skillful at representing the complexities of black urban adolescent life. These novels do not represent the white middle-class values that mainstream adolescent literature expresses, but the audiences of these urban texts have their life experiences affirmed by virtue of having quality writers to tell their stories.

Recent Works for Black Teen Audiences

The work of literary trailblazers such as Walter Dean Myers, Louise Meriwether, Rosa Guy, and Alice Childress set the stage for more contemporary authors such as Jacqueline Woodson, Christopher Paul Curtis, and Janet McDonald. While these newer authors continue the narrative of black adolescence in urban settings, they create stories with a few variations. For instance, Woodson's black characters are, by and large, middle class. If the characters in her work do not have middle-class origins, Woodson creates a situation whereby these characters encounter middle-class life in some way; *Maizon at Blue Hill* (1992) comes to mind here. Maizon is an academically gifted black teen who resides with her grandmother in a working-class neighborhood in Brooklyn. She is invited to attend an elite prep school, which places her in a middle-class environment. Although Maizon eventually decides to leave Blue Hill Academy, the fact that Woodson created such a situation for her character suggests that middle-class values are significant in the way she perceives enriching coming-of-age experiences. Christopher Paul Curtis is careful in his representations of blackness as well. His novel *Bud, not Buddy* tells the story of an eleven-year-old orphan, Bud Caldwell, during the Great Depression. While Bud travels throughout Michigan in search of someone whom he believes to be his father, he encounters moments of despair among other black people. However, once Bud locates his family, readers recognize that his life will change from being an orphan on the lam from the foster care system to a middle-class black boy who lives with his extended family.

In 2007, Coe Booth released a novel titled *Tyrell*.[8] Like McDonald, Booth's writing is loosely based on her coming-of-age experiences as a teen growing up in the Bronx. Moreover, Booth's work as an advocate for families in crisis is reflected in *Tyrell*. The protagonist of the novel, Tyrell Green, is fifteen, homeless, and the product of an irresponsible mother and an incarcerated, drug-dealing father. As a high school dropout, Tyrell spends most of his days worrying about his seven-year-old brother, Troy, and thinking about ways to make money so that his family can move out of the roach-infested homeless shelter where they are forced to live. Although his mother wants him to sell drugs to help feed and shelter the family, Tyrell does not want to get involved with illegal activity that will land him in jail. With no high school diploma, however, Tyrell's options are limited. In the end, Tyrell does not follow his mother's advice to become a drug dealer. Instead, he decides to throw a neighborhood party in order to raise money. The party scheme ultimately fails, but luckily, his family is able to leave the homeless shelter and move back into the projects. Tyrell's story reflects the reality of many urban teenagers. Young adult authors are creating stories that will fulfill the needs of readers who often live lives that are not reflected in mainstream literature.

New Jersey–based Townsend Press is a relatively new publisher of urban fiction marketed to young adult readers. The Bluford Series was created in order to provide accessible, but still sophisticated, reading for high school students. The first installment of the series, *Lost and Found*, was published in 2002, and as of 2007 there are currently thirteen novels in the series. The novels are no longer than two hundred pages and there is care taken to include both male and female protagonists in the storylines. It is important to note that the characters in the Bluford Series books are mostly African American and the setting of the novels is in the inner city. Named after the first African American astronaut, Guion "Guy" Bluford, and also for the name of the school that the characters in the series attend, the novels address relevant issues urban teens face. The Bluford Series is popular among adolescents, teachers, and parents because, while the writing style and the storylines are engaging, there need be no concern for censoring the books based on issues of bad language and inappropriate behavior on the characters' part. The series is also unique in that the books' cost is minimal: one dollar per novel. The teacher's guide is only three dollars. The affordability makes it possible for students to purchase the books on their own and for teachers to adopt the books for their classrooms.

Finally, while the characters in the Bluford Series face adversity as black urban teens, the authors of the books resist the tendency to portray these adolescents in stereotypical ways. Instead, whatever flaws the characters present, there is a counternarrative in the books that communicate solutions to the problems they face. For instance, in *Lost and Found*, the protagonist Darcy Willis's anger toward her father for abandoning his family causes her to ignore his parental advice about keeping away from older boys and the dangers of premature sexual activity. Darcy dismisses his advice and then ends up nearly getting raped by an older boy whom she has had a crush on. Mr. Willis arrives in time to rescue her from her predicament, which causes Darcy to reconsider her feelings about her father. While *Lost and Found* and the other books in the series are didactic in tone, they offer plausible insight into some of the challenges of coming of age as an urban teen.

McDonald's awareness of the character types that writers of black adolescent fiction create is concerned with class issues and the importance of survival. It also mattered to her that the characters in her work do more than just survive and that the readers of these novels reap the benefits of entertainment. McDonald wanted to create characters who become more than they are, by way of discovering their hidden talents. As in her memoir, the characters in the Project Girls Series and the Brother Hood Series all surpass the act of surviving. These characters demonstrate to readers the importance of hope and determination, in the sense that they are not born middle class and, thus, are without the innate skills of oppressing those whom they perceive to be less than them. Instead, those characters knock down roadblocks that are in place to exclude them from the rewards of upward mobility. McDonald does not present characters to readers who merely strive for middle-class status; her characters want respect based on their personal merits and talents. For instance, Raven does not dream of being rich and acquiring material goods. Instead, her mission is to utilize her strengths (intelligence) in order to change the conditions of her and her child's life. Aisha is not obsessed with wealth or materialism, nor is she enthralled with becoming famous. The fact that she becomes something of a celebrity allows her to support her family without having to work át menial jobs. Aisha's contract with Big Models Inc. is a means to an end.

The same can be said for Nate in *Brother Hood* and Hustle in *Harlem Hustle*. While Nate is a prep school student who, by virtue of his in-school social networks, can abandon his neighborhood life and friends, such is not his desire. Like most teens, Nate likes fashionable clothing and nice cars, but he doesn't worship these things. Moreover, he verges on disdain for middle-class and upper-middle-class existence. When his girlfriend, Willa Matthews, invites Nate and some of her other friends to meet her parents for a family dinner, Nate resents the performance acted out by the parents. The questioning regarding his family's educational and occupational status makes him uncomfortable, because Nate understands that Willa's parents are not merely making polite conversation; they are, instead, sizing him up in order to determine if he is good enough for their daughter and all of the social connections that come with association with the family. In response to the Matthews' remarks about the importance of class status, Nate responds by telling them:

> Having a bank account and a certain title does not make you superior. Being a good person does, and respecting where you come from and the people who are still there. That's what I admire more than . . . trappings. (*Brother Hood* 95)

While McDonald's novels do not always portray urban living in a positive light, McDonald is careful to point out some of the social concerns of those in the middle class. And sometimes, the middle class's flaws are exposed. Thus, while there is not a concern for neighborhood safety or issues of poverty within the representations of middle-class life, the work of urban-fiction writers makes considerable social commentary on the ideologies of exclusion that keep poor blacks and middle-class black people separate, if not physically, then socially. At the same time, however, unlike several of the novels from the uplift tradition, more contemporary black novelists do not create characters who long to climb socially in order to get away from lower-class black people, nor do these authors include characters that pass racially. Similarly, there is not a sense of complacency with the ills of urban life in these novels, nor do McDonald and other authors of black teen fiction romanticize poverty and crime.

One example is that of Eric Hustle Samson, in *Harlem Hustle*, who celebrates his community and at the same time looks for ways that he can be a positive contributor to his environment. As mentioned earlier, the novel begins with Hustle's connections to crime. Having been abandoned by his drug-addicted parents, Hustle initially knows no other way to survive except by stealing. While readers witness Hustle's efforts to elude police in his quest to make money by selling stolen goods, they also understand that Hustle does not have plans to lead a life of crime. Hustle does not particularly like traditional school and so is a high school dropout. However, Hustle has plans of becoming a rapper. This can be read as a pipe dream, but it connects Hustle to many readers who feel the same way about school, but who lack ideas about how to make their dreams come true in nontraditional ways. Hustle encounters the downside of the music industry. All is not fun and games in the quest to become a music artist; Hustle is assaulted and one of his songs is stolen from him by way of a bad contract that he was strong-armed into signing. Providing evidence to readers that every dream is fulfilled by perseverance and hard work takes the edge off the belief that it is easy to succeed in certain professions.

McDonald helps readers recognize that just because Hustle can rap does not guarantee his success in the music industry. To support her message, McDonald weaves within Hustle's story a standard admonition that almost every teen hears when they tell their parents that they want to be professional athletes or famous musicians: have a back-up plan. Hustle's advice comes from his girlfriend Jeannette's grandmother, who takes every opportunity to remind Hustle of the importance of schooling. It is no accident that Jeannette is portrayed as a prep school student and her grandmother is a retired teacher. Hustle is surrounded by traditional avenues from which to succeed. The difference, however, is that McDonald is careful not to exclude Hustle socially from these types of relationships. Just as Jeannette's family has something to offer Hustle, McDonald provides a way for Hustle to reveal his strengths.

Shades of the Ghetto

The creation of the character Cameron Storm, in *Off-Color*, comes from McDonald's memories of a distant cousin and a graduate school friend who both were black, but looked white. McDonald's previous work looks at race as a significant factor in coming of age, but not until *Off-Color* does McDonald address racial issues head on. One characteristic of urban fiction is that race, as it is viewed from an outsider's perspective, is not a major concern of the black characters. In fact, rarely are there white characters in urban novels, and if they do exist, they are portrayed in token roles or as marginal characters who serve to disturb the overall environment of the text. As a result of the inward focus of McDonald's novels, the characters in her fiction do not ruminate over their race in terms of intraracial concerns with skin tone as it relates to social status. In fact, none of her characters mention their race as being a factor in how they feel about themselves. Instead, other cultural markers matter more. Family, home, leisure activities, and work are examined in terms of how these adolescent characters mark their racial identity.

Urban fiction, McDonald's novels included, presents realistic portraits of family in terms of the numerous possibilities of configuration. For the most part, these families are headed by single women, who were either never married or were abandoned by the father of their children. While these portrayals can be read as negative representations of the black family, the fact remains that single female–headed households are prevalent in urban areas. As a result, to have the characters in her novels obsess over their family makeup is unrealistic. McDonald includes two-parent families such as her own in *Project Girl*, Jesse

Honoré's in *Spellbound*, and Nate's in *Brother Hood*. Readers come to understand that single-parent households are just as diverse as two-parent households. McDonald grew up in a working-class family with her postal worker father. McDonald's family remained in Farragut Homes despite the fact that most of the two-parent residents had been replaced by single-parent families. McDonald's situation is not uncommon, although the rhetoric regarding family structure and economics states that two-parent homes are usually better than single-parent homes. Considering that Mrs. McDonald did not work outside the home and Mr. McDonald's salary did not amount to enough to support a middle-class lifestyle, the McDonalds remained in the working class. Jesse Honoré, in *Spellbound*, lives with his lawyer mother and high school principal father. His older sister is away at college and his parents look forward to the day when he, too, makes it to college. Despite the fact that Jesse lives in a comfortable home with all of the advantages of parents who are upwardly mobile and wise in the ways of advocating for their children, it does not stop Jesse from falling into the downward spiral of teen parenting. Nate's family is similar to Janet's, in that the Whitelys are working class. Unlike the McDonalds, however, the Whiteleys are not as concerned about where they live; they are more focused on the futures of their sons. Nate's older brother struggles with his status in the Whitely family and focuses on creating a separate identity for himself that is opposite that of his brother Nate. The Whitelys are consumed with Eli's well-being in that his decision making increasingly affects the entire family. They understand the significance of race in terms of Eli's potential dealings with the police; however, there is not an explicit discussion regarding racial inequality or intraracial prejudice. Similarly, Nate's conflict with his girlfriend Willa stems not from Nate's friends being black, but from her expectations for Nate to behave middle class when he is with her. All of her comments regarding Nate's friends, though consistent with black lifestyles and fashion, are based on her socioeconomic background rather than her blackness. In each of these cases, McDonald's characters do not lament about being black; instead, they navigate their lives in terms of how to gain personal success and freedom for themselves and those within their extended family.

It is not until Cameron Storm, in *Off-Color*, that McDonald provides an encounter with racial hierarchies and shows how those structures help to communicate to adolescents their position in society. As mentioned earlier, before she discovers that she is biracial Cameron is able to construct a positive view of herself, but her vision is based on the denigration of black people. Although Cameron's family is working class, she does not view herself as poor; she eschews the behaviors of the poor students in her school and in her community, as she categorizes their actions as specifically black. In this sense, while Cameron's financial status is identical, if not lower, than the black poor people around her, she unconsciously sees herself as economically and socially superior due to her whiteness. McDonald's narrative structure helps readers recognize that Cameron does not come by her understanding of race and class by accident. Instead, her daily involvement with those unlike her is limited. Like many nonminority children, Cameron gets her information about the "other" from the media. Since blackness is often equated with poverty, Cameron concludes that the project girls are poor and thus lack social graces. In mainstream classrooms and those portrayed in literature, rarely do students get exposure to diverse populations. More often than not, exposure to diversity comes in the form of isolated lessons about famous minority figures who represent the exceptions to stereotypical beliefs about black people; for example, February's Black History Month is a time when children across the country learn about a few "heroes" of black culture and history. In the classroom scene in *Off-Color*, McDonald gives readers insight into how, while Shakespeare's *Othello* is a canonical text, it is possible to expose students to classical literature that is relevant to their lives, rather than merely providing a summary of the basic plot.

The method of studying difference in isolation prevents both minority and nonminority students from absorbing more than just a cursory knowledge of difference. These so-called heroes do not in fact convince struggling black children that they, too, are an important part of making history through social change, nor do they convince nonminority children that the talents and genius of a particular hero are part and parcel of the same capabilities of their minority classmates. One of the dilemmas black writers of children's and adolescent literature face is how to change the dissemination of incorrect information about black people while entertaining their readers. So far, the solution has been for black authors to share their stories in the form of nonfiction. Much of the children's and adolescent literature for and about black people is published in the form of short biographies. The focus on changing the minds of nonminorities means that black children and young adults find themselves in search of more entertaining literature than the heavy-handed biographies written about people and places they find distant and more academic than pleasurable.

Since so much of the literature that is written for black adolescents is purpose driven, in the sense that texts are most often used as a vehicle for racial change, very little space is left in these works to explore the living environment and lifestyles of the characters. Moreover, since the authors of literature from the uplift tradition had a mission to reeducate readers about race, rarely did child characters have a prominent voice in the work. McDonald's approach to storytelling, however, addresses these elements by weaving the physical and social environment into her stories and by positioning the adult characters in her books as secondary in order to give the adolescent characters the primary voice. For instance, the Project Girls Series gives readers a different perspective on public housing and its residents than does the beginning of Cameron's narrative about the projects. It is not until Cameron becomes a project girl herself that she is able to see the lives of those she mocked from a different vantage point. In the Brother Hood Series, Nate and Hustle give readers a picture of Harlem through a lens of the places and people that concern them personally. These adolescent perspectives address the ingredients that make up their urbanness and their blackness. McDonald's characters help readers understand how adolescents define race; this definition does not focus on skin color more than the total makeup of the characters' lives. In the more purpose-driven literature the personal lives of teenagers are deemed inconsequential to the larger concerns of the status of the entire race. These novels did not take into account the perspective of adolescents, and thus purpose-driven literature does not touch teen readers in the same way as the more contemporary works of writers such as McDonald.

Given the ongoing concern for the importance of how blackness is represented to those outside the race and culture, it is no wonder that urban-centered novels face challenges in mainstream settings. However, just as scholars and teachers of adolescent literature assert that all teens need literature that speaks to their lives, these readers must also, on a regular basis, encounter works that include characters and voices that do not match their racial and cultural experience. McDonald's work provides such a lens.

Notes

1. "Up the Down Staircase: Where Snoop and Shakespeare Meet." *Horn Book* (November–December 2005): 747–51.

2. Quoted in bell hooks, *Bone Black: Memories of Girlhood* (New York: Henry Holt, 1996), xii.

3. Rudine Sims-Bishop, *Presenting Walter Dean Myers* (Boston: Twayne, 1991).

4. While the definition of the term *urban* is dependent upon location and demographics, for the purposes of this discussion, *urban* is used in the context of hip-hop cultural and literary traditions of black people. The authors discussed in this section are black and their focus is on their experiences as black writers.

5. See Dorothy Broderick, *Image of the Black in Children's Fiction* (New York: R. R. Bowker Co., 1973); Rudine Sims-Bishop, *Shadow and Substance Afro-American Experience in Contemporary Children's Fiction* (Urbana, IL: National Council of Teachers of English, c1982); Donnarae MacCann, *White Supremacy in Children's Literature: Characterizations of African Americans, 1830–1900* (New York: Garland, 1998).

6. Victoria C. Murphy, "Triple Crown Winner: In the Hot Category of Urban Fiction, Ex-Offender Victoria Springer Self-Published Her Story and Launched Her Successful, Independent Press." *Black Issues Book Review* 6, no. 3 (May–July 2004): 28.

7. From http://streetfiction.org/?page_id=8 (accessed). March 20, 2007.

8. Coe Booth, *Tyrell* (New York: Push, 2007).

CHAPTER SEVEN

~

I Write Stories
with Happy Endings

There is a growing body of memoirs being written by black authors who revisit their adolescence, as well as an increasing amount of black adolescent–focused literature. McDonald's *Project Girl* is in good company with memoirs such as Charlise Lyles' *Do I Dare Disturb the Universe?* (1994) and Debra Dickerson's *An American Story* (2000). Lyles' coming-of-age experience is similar to McDonald's in that her family was one of the founding residents of the former Kennedy-King Homes in Cleveland, Ohio. Lyles and her siblings encountered the same roadblocks as the McDonald siblings; however, in her memoir, Lyles presents her understanding of her coming-of-age journey more from an outward perspective, in which she frames her life's course through the turbulent times of the 1960s and 1970s. Readers get an oral history of the struggles of black Cleveland residents: rising black unemployment, the pitfalls of urban schooling, the declining environment of public housing, and political upheaval.

Debra Dickerson's *An American Story* differs from Lyles' and McDonald's memoirs in that her focus seems to be placed on how she was able to assimilate into middle-class American culture. Up until her early adolescence, Dickerson was raised in a conservative two-parent home where rules were strict and expectations high. Like Lyles and McDonald, Dickerson was identified as academically talented and thus sent to a school outside of her neighborhood. She eventually graduated from college and entered the United States Navy, where she achieved an officer's rank. Dickerson's narrative points readers toward the ways in which one can make himself or herself acceptable to those who hold power in order to become a power holder as well. Dickerson's narrative is not overly concerned about racial issues, other than that her words communicate to readers the belief that one's redeeming qualities can help transcend the confines of prejudice.

A similar narrative with a black adolescent male perspective is Ron Suskind's *A Hope in the Unseen* (1998). In *Hope*, Suskind charts the journey of Cedric Jennings, an inner-city youth from a single-parent home who dares to use his academic gifts to escape poverty and social isolation. While still in high school, Cedric survives near homelessness and intense scrutiny from his peers. In a review of *Hope*, Janet McDonald remarks, "The throat-tightening fear that one feels in one's own neighborhood, a place that should feel like home, comes across all too effectively. The menacing gang members in school and dangerous drug dealers just outside leave Cedric few oases of peace other than home, empty classrooms or church."[1] Like McDonald, once he leaves his old neighborhood for college, Cedric quickly realizes that in order to be successful at an Ivy League institution, he needs to reeducate himself in terms of the social protocols of a university environment.

By no means an exhaustive list of urban youth memoirs, these are representative of a familiar pattern in black adolescents' lives. To begin with, the stereotype about black anti-intellectualism among black adolescents is exploded by the stories these memoirs tell. A common thread in the narratives is the parents' quest for a solid and uplifting education for their children. For the most part, such a dream is realized until these teens enter adolescence. Once in their teens, the narratives in black coming-of-age memoirs shift from bliss to chaos. With age comes wisdom and understanding and thus the once comfortable world of childhood is exposed to these writers as merely a temporary condition.

Another common theme in black coming-of-age narratives is the time and place where the shift from living in the comfort and safety of one's community is redirected, under the guise of providing a better education for the teen, to the harsh realities of racism and classism that undermine confidence. Taken out of their communities, these teens discover the inequities of social and economic hierarchies. The disappointment arrives when they discover that the world of privilege is not meant for minorities. The recognition of the barriers to achieving the American Dream by these authors then becomes the focus of their work. Authors such as McDonald, Dickerson, Lyles, and Jennings (Suskind) remind readers that social and economic change exacts an extraordinary price and often that cost comes in the form of the sacrificing of the old self in order to construct or resocialize a new self.

Furthermore, what marks these narratives as pertinent to black adolescent readers is the fact that while not all black teens live in harsh neighborhoods infested by poverty, crime, and illiteracy, black teens face special circumstances based on the color of their skin. The historical legacy of racism ensures that no matter where these teens grow up, there is always the task before them of reinventing themselves into an identity that is not threatening to dominant culture. Often, black teens are not aware of the depths to which they must go in order to achieve a level of acceptance and that they will never gain total acceptance by the dominant society. Instead, the concern over being examined as a collective rather than as an individual is foremost in these teens' minds, and there is an unspoken responsibility to be a "credit" to the race, or in Du Boisian terms, to show the "best of blackness." Coupled with their particular family codes regarding self-presentation and racial discretion, there is always the admonishment of "twice as good to get half as much" that many black youth grow up hearing.

McDonald's narratives are consistent with the struggles that most black teens will face in their quest to be more and do more with their lives. In all of her work, McDonald infuses the notion that personal and professional growth can be accomplished in numerous ways if teens are led to the knowledge that they must first uncover their personal strengths. Adults can help adolescents feel better about themselves if there is an understanding that there is no such thing as a universal adolescence. Instead, teens' decisions about their future are often based on the past trajectory of their lives. In other words, teens use what they know to get by.

Janet McDonald lived and wrote about what she knew—making it. In our last conversation, I asked her to make a few summative remarks about her work. She shared, "I do not write books for adults. If adults read my books and get something from them, that is great. When I write, I am speaking to children and adolescents. I want my readers to understand that what they need to do is to keep keepin' on, no matter what." McDonald went on to explain that her mission is not to provide readers with fairy tales, nor does she aim to depress them. Instead, her mission is to give voice to real situations that teens face. McDonald's early experience with literature and reading is what influenced her own writing. She recognized that within the genre of adolescent literature, the black-adolescent voice did not speak as it should. Her understanding of the structure and content of prototypical adolescent texts helped her to understand why assumptions are often made about the content and quality of adolescent literature. Throughout her adolescence, McDonald read canonical texts. It was not until college that she learned that not all authors were, in fact, white, male, and dead. Her newfound knowledge meant that she expanded her reading tastes to include a more diverse range of reading materials. Yet, she was not a reader of adolescent literature.

Embedded in her characters' actions is McDonald's belief in faith, hope, and perseverance. Her characters encounter seemingly impossible odds, yet they prevail in their own way. McDonald's own life is proof that mistakes do not have to be the end of a future for teens; the characters embody this belief. What is important to notice, however, is that while the characters demonstrate her commitment to moving forward with life, McDonald believed that the road to triumph is not the same for us all. She grew up poor and in the projects; it took her longer than most to complete her college degrees; she suffered trauma and thus her emotional status was compromised. Yet, despite all of those incidents, she achieved success. Although she believed in second and sometimes third chances, McDonald did not intend for her work to possess the maudlin tone of a Hallmark card. She also believed in being "real." This realness meant that her work must contain honesty—the type of candidness that sometimes put her at odds with her critics. To begin with, all of the novels are set in urban areas. While her characters travel in various circles—Raven at college, Nate in prep school, and Aisha on Manhattan's Fifth Avenue—they hold on to their urban roots. None of her characters live affluent lives, which is in keeping with her intended readership. All of the characters, however, are bright in their own way. Never does she portray a teen who does not want to learn. Although Aisha does not care for the confines of a traditional classroom, she has the intellectual skills that give her the power to manage her own world, while at the same time contributing to others' worlds, as she does in *Spellbound* when she helps Raven study for the spelling bee. Even in the case of Eric Samson in *Harlem Hustle*, Mc-Donald represents a measure of intellectual adeptness in her characters. In the beginning of the novel, it's no secret that Eric dislikes school. By the novel's end, readers learn that it is not that Eric is illiterate or lazy; instead, as with Aisha, traditional schooling does not address Eric's learning style and educational needs.

It is not that McDonald considers her sole audience to be from urban working-class and poor environments; instead, she wants to give voice to a segment of the adolescent population that rarely gets to speak: ordinary urban youth who find their way in a world that is often unforgiving to those who are different. At the same time, McDonald reminds us that her stories, though filled with black protagonists, share a universal appeal to all teen readers around the world who battle adolescent angst, struggle with romance, school, adults, and numerous other challenges that teens face on a daily basis. Who would have thought that a project girl would become a Vassar graduate and an international corporate lawyer? Similarly, who would believe that a young black male with baggy jeans and a do-rag is also a Dostoevsky-reading, prep school student? McDonald's providing of foils to the popular stereotypical images of urban youth is a powerful strategy for expanding the readers' views of themselves. Hopefully, these contradictory images of black teens can act as a mirror to reflect readers' undiscovered potential. Moreover, McDonald's characters are not portrayed in an overly hip and cool manner that would lead readers to assess them as inauthentic and contrived. Raven is bookish, but she is not infallible in some of the challenges that come with adolescence. Hustle is a cool street kid who has had dealings with the law, but he possesses the tender qualities that make him silently long for a family of his own. All of the characters are talented, though some, like the Washington sisters, take longer than usual to finish high school. All of the characters want to know who they are and where they come from. Cameron makes it her primary goal to define herself on her own terms once she learns that her identity is more complex than she could have ever imagined. McDonald does not create superheroes or religious figures. Her characters, like her readers, are ordinary. However, what makes them special is the fact that none of them give up on life.

Because it was McDonald's mission to create hope and happy endings for her readers, she contemplated leaving any mention of her illness out of this book. Reviewers criticize the endings in several of her novels. *Chill Wind*, with its protagonist Aisha, is the most frequent target. For instance, a *Publishers Weekly* reviewer contends that "her [Aisha's] mother quits drinking, and this, coupled with her sudden bonding with her sister, add to the improbable ending. In the end, with things coming so easily to Aisha, readers will be left wondering what she has learned along the way." McDonald asks her critics, "Why not happy endings for black teens?"[2] She wanted to prevail over her illness, though quietly, and then go on with the rest of her life. Moreover, she wanted to hold true to her belief that anything is possible. McDonald was, in short, puzzled by her misfortune; during the early stages of her illness, she spent countless hours researching traditional and holistic cures for her disease. She joined several online communities where battlers and survivors of cancer share their feelings and concerns. Her goal was to maintain a sense of hope by learning about those who had survived and have important information for those still in the struggle. McDonald was not ready to let cancer take her life. She wrote that when she was in the early stages of her illness, she did not take seriously the gravity of her condition. So many people beat cancer, she explained. In fact, shortly after her initial diagnosis of cancer in September 2005, McDonald was busy on the road attending conferences and celebrating the success of *Brother Hood*. As the illness wore on, fear replaced courage, but defeat was never an option. By 2006, McDonald's illness showed signs of progression, yet through the chronic exhaustion she suffered as a result of her treatment, she made it a point to attend the National Teachers of English Convention in Nashville in order to present at the Assembly on Literature for Adolescents (ALAN) Conference. There, McDonald gave what turns out to be her last large-scale public lecture. In her talk, McDonald shared her ultimate purpose for writing novels for adolescent audiences: "I write books that I wish were around when I was fifteen and staring into the mirror going 'eww!!'"[3]

Janet during the early stages of her illness.

Janet's physical appearance suggests that her illness is increasingly becoming a challenge to her once-super-energetic spirit.

McDonald's life had been filled with challenges. Her last challenge, a diagnosis of cancer, topped all the others. Janet talked at length about how that news impacted her life and her writing. As with most people who battle the disease, the physical toll on the body often drives the emotional state of the patient. McDonald expressed that throughout her illness, she went through phases of asking "Why me?" to resolving to beat the illness. She held out hope that her disease was merely a setback in her life and, considering all that she had been through, surely she would survive being ill.

Notes

1. Review from August 1998 Salon.com, accessed March 20, 2007.

2. Janet McDonald, interview by Catherine Ross-Stroud, Paris, March 13, 2007.

3. Janet McDonald. "Young Adult Literature: Key to Open Minds." Paper presented at annual Assembly on Literature for Adolescents workshop, Nashville, TN, November 20–21, 2006.

~

Epilogue

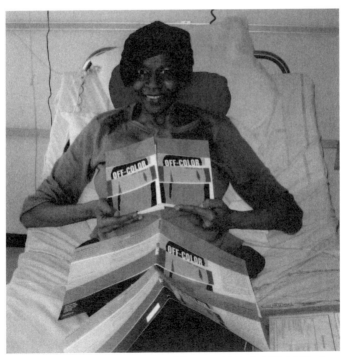

Janet at Hôpital Universaitaite Paul-Brousse 2007, in Villejuif Cedex.

On April 11, 2007, Janet A. McDonald passed away at the age of fifty-three. Throughout her battle, McDonald had a close network of friends to rely on for support. One of those friends confronted McDonald with a question concerning her reservations about mentioning her battle with cancer for this book. This person reminded her that if she was as committed to being "real" and telling the truth as is contended in her work, then she must hold on to the truth with the same vigor in her own life.

It is with the truth in mind that McDonald mused aloud, "If I have been saved from so much, how can it be that cancer is going to take me? I survived trauma. I survived depression. Some of the risks that I have taken along the way should have meant the end of my life, but that did not happen. I am still here and I am grateful for every day that I am alive. I write stories for teenagers in order to give them hope. I write stories with happy endings. I do not write sad endings . . . the kind where the protagonist dies."[1]

Note

1. Telephone communication.

~

References

Primary Sources

Memoir
McDonald, Janet. *Project Girl*. New York: Farrar, Straus and Giroux, 1999.

Young Adult Novels by Janet McDonald
Spellbound. New York: Farrar, Straus and Giroux, 2001.
Chill Wind. New York: Farrar, Straus and Giroux, 2002.
Twists and Turns. New York: Farrar, Straus and Giroux, 2003.
Brooklyn Babies. Translated into French by Nathalie Zimmerman. Paris: Thierry Magnier, 2003.
Brother Hood. New York: Farrar, Straus and Giroux, 2004.
Top-Rondes. Translated into French by Nathalie Zimmerman. Paris: Thierry Magnier, 2004.
Harlem Hustle, New York: Farrar, Straus and Giroux, 2006.
Des Tift et du Taf. Translated into French by Nathalie Zimmerman. Paris: Thierry Magnier, 2006.
Frères de rap. Translated into French by Nathalie Zimmerman. Paris: Thierry Magnier, 2007.
Off-Color. New York: Farrar, Straus and Giroux, 2007.

Articles, Columns, Etc. by Janet McDonald

"Dear Shawnda." In *Dear Author: Letters of Hope*. Edited by Joan F. Kaywell. New York: Philomel, 2007, 133–34.

"Double Life." *Literary Review: An International Journal of Contemporary Writing* 45, no. 4 (Summer 2002): 679–84.

"X-Patriate." *Literary Review* 47, no. 1, 2003: 58–62.

"Project Girls: Five Veterans of the City's Public Housing Tell Their Stories." *Village Voice* (January 16, 2001): 58–64.

"A Sister in Paris: American African Woman in Paris, France." *Essence Magazine* 25, no. 1 (May 1, 1994): 54.

Interviews

Engberg, Gillian. "Booklist Interview." *Booklist* 98, no. 12 (February 15, 2002): 1026.

Farrar, Straus, Giroux. Interview with Janet McDonald. www.fsgkidsbooks.com/audiovideo.htm March 20, 2007.

Follos, Alison M. G. "Janet McDonald: Big Up Brooklyn! Bridging Cultures." *Library Media Connection* 24, no. 3 (November–December 2005): 42–44.

Kennedy, Thomas E. "Up from Brooklyn: An Interview with Janet McDonald." *Literary Review: An International Journal of Contemporary Writing* 44, no. 4 (2001): 704–20.

Ross-Stroud, Catherine. Interview with Janet McDonald. Paris, March 13, 2007.

Williams, Jennifer. *"Twists and Turns: An Interview with Janet McDonald."* *Hip Mama*, October 2003. *http://www.hipmama.com/node/197 March 20, 2007.*

Media Appearances

Rosie O'Donnell Show. NBC Studios, New York. March 1999.

Leeza. NBC Studios, Los Angeles. March 1999.

Glass, Ira. "Notes of a Native Daughter." *An American Life*. Chicago Public Radio. August 24, 2001.

"Young Adult Literature: Key to Open Minds." Paper presented at annual Assembly on Literature for Adolescents workshop, Nashville, TN, November 20–21, 2006.

Criticism and Essays by Janet McDonald

"Author Talk: Bad Language." *Voices of Youth Advocates Online* (August 2005).

"Up the Down Staircase: Where Snoop and Shakespeare Meet." *Horn Book* (November–December 2005): 747–51.

Short Story by Janet McDonald
"Zebra Girl." In *Skin Deep: Stories that Cut to the Bone*. Edited by Tony Bradman. London: Puffin, 2004.

Review by Janet McDonald
"Black Like (White) Me." A Review of *A Hope in the Unseen* by Ronald Suskind." Salon.com www.salon.com/mwt/feature/1998/08/cov_24feature.html (August 24, 1998).

Secondary Sources

Biographical Sources
Engberg, Gillian. "Sad news." (Janet McDonald Obituary) *Booklist* 103, no. 18 (May 15, 2007): 42.

Farrar, Straus, Giroux Books for Young Readers Biographical Information Website, http://www.fsgkidsbooks.com/authordetails.asp?ID=McDonald March 20, 2007.

Follos, Alison M. G. "Janet McDonald: Farewell to a YA Talent." *Library Media Connection* 26, no. 1 (August–September 2007): 45.

"Janet McDonald." In *Something about the Author*. Vol. 148. Detroit: Gale, 155–57.

Powers, Retha. "Janet McDonald 1953–2007: Make Some Noise for the Project Girl." *Black Issues Book Review* 9, no. 3 (May–June 2007): 33.

Reillihan, Heather. "Janet McDonald." In *African American Biographers: A Sourcebook*. Edited by Emmanuel Nelson. Westport, CT: Greenwood, 2002.

Selected Book Reviews

Project Girl
Black Issues Book Review (March–April 1999): 52.

Booklist 95, no. 7 (December 1, 1998): 649.

"Forecasts: Nonfiction," *Publishers Weekly* 245, no. 47 (November 23, 1998): 28–29.

Hayes, Arthur. "The Thin Black Line." American Bar Association (April 1999): 81–82.

Library Journal 123, no. 18 (November 1, 1998): 97.

New York Times Book Review (February 1999): 17.

Quart, Lenny. "Letter from New York: Growing Up in the Projects." *American Studies Today* Online, http://www.americansc.org.uk/Online/Projects.htm September 30, 2005.

Tekulve, Susan. "Review of *Project Girl*, by Janet McDonald," *Literary Review: An International Journal of Contemporary Writing* 44 (4) (Summer 2001): 799.

Time 153, no. 8 (March 1, 1999): 81.

Spellbound

Beram, Nell D. "Spellbound. " *Horn Book* 78, no. 1 (January–February 2002): 80.

Booklist 98, no. 13 (March 15, 2002): 1228.

Engberg, G., and H. Rochman. *Booklist* 98, no. 12 (February 15, 2002): 1028.

Goldsmith, Francisca. *School Library Journal* 47, no. 9 (September 2001): 230.

Journal of Adolescent & Adult Literacy 47, no. 3 (November 2003): 216.

Kirkus Reviews 69, no. 20 (October 15, 2001): 1488.

Publishers Weekly 248, no. 47 (November 19, 2001): 68.

Publishers Weekly 250, no. 48 (December 1, 2003): 59.

Chill Wind

ALAN Review 33, no. 3 (July 2006): 134.

Booklist 99, no. 5 (November 1, 2002): 485.

Booklist 99, no. 12 (February 15, 2003): 1083.

Horn Book Magazine 78.5 (September–October 2002): 576.

Journal of Adolescent & Adult Literacy 48, no. 3 (November 2004): 253.

Kirkus Reviews 70, no. 19 (October 1, 2002): 1475.

Kliatt 40, no. 3 (May 2006): 21.

Publishers Weekly 249, no. 45 (November 11, 2002): 65.

School Librarian 52, no. 3 (Autumn 2004): 159.

School Library Journal 48, no. 11 (November 2002): 173.

Twists and Turns

Booklist 99, no. 21 (July 1, 2003): 1886.

Booklist 100, no. 9–10 (January 1, 2004): 779.

Horn Book 79, no. 5 (September–October 2003): 614.

Kirkus Reviews 71, no. 14 (July 15, 2003): 966.
Kliatt 40, no. 5 (September 2006): 26.
Library Media Connection 22, no. 6 (2004): 68.
Publishers Weekly 250, no. 34 (August 25, 2003): 66.
School Library Journal 49, no. 9 (September 2003): 217.

Brother Hood
Booklist 101, no. 1 (September 1, 2004): 108.
Horn Book 81, no. 1 (January–February 2005): 96.
Horn Book 82, no. 5 (September–October 2006): 592.
Journal of Adolescent & Adult Literacy 48, no. 4 (December 2004): 353.
Kirkus Reviews 72, no. 15 (August 1, 2004): 745.
Kliatt 38, no. 5 (September 1, 2004): 14.
School Library Journal 50, no. 11 (November 2004): 149.

Harlem Hustle
ALAN Review 4, no. 1 (Fall 2006).
Booklist 103, no. 7 (December 1, 2006): 39.
Bulletin of the Center for Children's Books 60, no. 5 (January 2007): 221.
Horn Book 82, no. 5 (September–October 2006): 592.
Kirkus Reviews 74, no. 19 (October 1, 2006): 1020.
Sciandra, Denise. "Letters to the Editor." *Horn Book* 82, no. 6 (November–December 2006): 372.
School Library Journal 52, no. 10 (October 2006): 161.

Off-Color
ALAN Review 35, no. 2 (January 1, 2008): 163.
Booklist 103, no. 22 (2007): 70–71.
Journal of Adolescent & Adult Literacy 51, no. 6 (May 1, 2008): 520–521.
Kirkus Reviews 75, no. 19 (October 1, 2007): 1052.
Kliatt 41, no. 6 (November 1, 2007): 12.
Publishers Weekly 254, no. 44 (November 5, 2007): 64–65.
School Library Journal 54, no. 3 (March 1, 2008): 204.

Other Sources

Anderson, Sheila. *Extreme Teens: Library Services to Nontraditional Young Adults.* Westport, CT: Libraries Unlimited, 2005.

Booth, Coe. *Tyrell*. New York: Push, 2006.

Broderick, Dorothy. *Image of the Black in Children's* Fiction. New York: R. R. Bowker Co., 1973.

Cart, Michael. *From Romance to Realism: 50 Years of Growth in Young Adult Literature*. New York: HarperCollins, 1996.

Chang, Jeff. *Can't Stop Won't Stop: A History of the Hip-Hop Generation*. New York: St. Martin's Press, 2005.

Crane, Diana. *Fashion and Its Social Agendas: Class, Gender, and Identity in Clothing*. Chicago: University of Chicago Press, 2000.

Cross, William. *Shades of Black: Diversity in African-American Identity*. Philadelphia: Temple University Press, 1991.

DeParle, Jason. *American Dream: Three Women, Ten Kids, and a Nation's Drive to End Welfare*. New York: Viking, 2004.

Dickerson, Debra. *An American Story*. New York: Pantheon, 2000.

Du Bois, W. E. B. *The Souls of Black Folk*. New York: Vintage, 1990.

Dyson, Micheal Eric. *Is Bill Cosby Right?: or Has the Black Middle Class Lost Its Mind?* New York: Civitas Books, 2005.

Egoff, Sheila. *Thursday's Child: Patterns and Trends in Contemporary Children's Literature*. Chicago: American Library Association, 1981.

Esmail, Ashraf, and Jas Sullivan. "African American College Males and Females: A Look at Color Mating Preferences." *Race, Class, Gender* 13, no. 1–2 (Winter 2006): 201–20.

Fordham, Signithia. *Blacked Out: Dilemmas of Race, Identity, and Success at Capital High*. Chicago: University of Chicago Press, 1996.

Gallo, Donald R. "Listening to Readers: Attitudes Toward the Young Adult Novel." In *Reading Their World: The Young Adult Novel in the Classroom*. Edited by Virginia Monseau and Gary Salvner. Portsmouth, NH: Boynton Cook, 1992.

Genette, Gérard. *Narrative Discourse: An Essay in Method*. Ithaca, NY: Cornell University Press, 1980.

Gilligan, Carol. *In a Different Voice: Psychological Theory of Women's Development*. Cambridge, MA: Harvard University Press, 1993.

Harris, Anita. *Future Girl: Young Women in the Twenty-First Century*. New York: Routledge, 2004.

Hinton-Johnson, KaaVonia. "Subverting Beauty Aesthetics in African-American Young Adult Literature." *Multicultural Review* 14, no. 2 (Summer 2005): 28–35.

hooks, bell. *Bone Black: Memories of Girlhood*. New York: Henry Holt, 1996.

Hunter, Margaret. *Race, Gender, and the Politics of Skin Tone*. New York: Routledge, 2005.

———. *Teaching to Transgress: Education as the Practice of Freedom.* New York: Routledge, 1994.

Johnson-Feelings, Dianne. *Telling Tales: The Pedagogy and Promise of Afro-American Literature for Youth.* New York: Greenwood Press, 1990.

Jones, LeAlan, and L. Newman. *Our America: Life and Death on the South Side of Chicago.* New York: Scribner, 1997.

Kelly, Patricia. "Youth as an Artifact of Expertise: Problematizing the Practice of Youth Studies in an Age of Uncertainty." *Journal of Youth Studies* 3, no. 3 (September 2000): 301–15.

Kenny, Lorraine. *Daughters of Suburbia: Growing Up White, Middle Class, and Female.* New Brunswick, NJ: Rutgers, 2000.

Lake, Obigele. *Blue Veins and Kinky Hair: Naming and Color Consciousness in African America.* Westport, CT: Praeger, 2003.

LeSeur, Geta. *Ten is the Age of Darkness: The Black Bildungsroman.* Columbia: University of Missouri Press, 1995.

Lyles, Charlise. *Do I Dare to Disturb the Universe?: From the Projects to Prep School.* New York: Faber and Faber, 1994.

MacCann, Donnarae. *White Supremacy in Children's Literature: Characterizations of African Americans, 1830–1900.* New York : Garland, 1998.

McWhorter, John. *All About The Beat: Why Hip-hop Can't Save Black America.* New York: Gotham Books, 2008.

Meloni, Christine. "Attracting New Readers with Hip-Hop Lit." *Library Media Connection* (February 2007): 38–40.

Monseau, Virginia, and Gary Salvner. *Reading Their World: The Young Adult Novel in the Classroom.* Portsmouth, NH: Boynton-Cook, 1992.

Murphy, Victoria C. "Triple Crown Winner: In the Hot Category of Urban Fiction, Ex-Offender Victoria Springer Self-Published Her Story and Launched Her Successful, Independent Press." *Black Issues Book Review* 6, no. 3 (May–July 2004): 28.

Neal-Barnett, A. M. "Being Black: A New Conceptualization of Acting White." In *Forging Links: African American Children Clinical Developmental Perspectives.* Edited by A. M. Neal-Barnett, J. Contreras, and K. Kerns. Westport, CT: Greenwood Publishing, 2001, 75–88.

Nodelman, Perry, and Mavis Reimer. *The Pleasures of Children's Literature.* 3rd edition. Boston: Allyn and Bacon, 2003.

Peck, David. *Novels of Initiation: A Guidebook for Teaching Literature to Adolescents.* New York: Teachers College Press, 1989.

Pluviose, David. "Study: 'Acting White' Accusation has Damaging Legacy for Black Students." *Diverse: Issues in Higher Education* 23 (4) (April 6, 2006): 8.

Poston, Walter. "The Biracial Identity Development Model: A Needed Addition." *Journal of Counseling and Development* (69) (1990): 152–55.

Reay, Diane. "Mostly Roughs and Toughs: Social Class, Race and Representation in Inner City Schooling." *Sociology* 38, no. 5 (December 2004): 1005–23.

Reillihan, Heather. "Janet McDonald." In *African American Biographers: A Sourcebook*. Edited by Emmanuel Nelson. Westport, CT: Greenwood Press, 2002.

Ross-Stroud, Catherine. "Non-Existent Existences: Race, Class, Gender, and Age in Adolescent Fiction; Or Those Whispering Black Girls." *Dissertation Abstracts International Website, Section A: The Humanities and Social Sciences* 64, no. 9 (2004): 3297, accessed March 20, 2007.

Saxton, Ruth O., ed. *The Girl: Constructions of the Girl in Contemporary Fiction by Women*. New York: St. Martin's, 1998.

Scales-Trent, J. 1995. *Notes of a White Black Woman: Race, Color Community*. University Park: Pennsylvania State University Press.

Schraff, Ann. *Lost and Found*. West Berlin, NJ: Townsend Press, 2002.

Sharpiro, Ann-Louise. *Housing the Poor of Paris*. Madison: University of Wisconsin Press, 1985.

Sims-Bishop, Rudine. *Shadow and Substance: Afro-American Experience in Contemporary Children's Fiction*. Urbana, IL: National Council of Teachers of English, 1982.

———. *Presenting Walter Dean Myers*. Boston: Twayne Publishers, 1991.

Smith, Craig. "Inside French Housing Project, Feelings of Being the Outsiders," *New York Times*, November 9, 2005, p. 1A.

Smith, Karen Patricia. *African-American Voices in Young Adult Literature: Tradition, Transition, Transformation*. Lanham, MD: Scarecrow Press, 1994.

Smitherman, Geneva. *Talkin' and Testifyin': The Language of Black America*. New York: Routledge, 2000.

———. *Word from the Mother: Language and African Americans*. New York: Routledge, 2006.

Stephens, John, H. *Language and Ideology in Children's Fiction*. United Kingdom and New York: Longman, 1992.

Stossel, John. "Skin Deep Discrimination: Colorism Shows We're a Long Way from a Color-Blind Society." *20/20*, ABC. March 4, 2005.

Stover, Lois, and Eileen Tway. "Cultural Diversity and the Young Adult Novel." In *Reading Their World: The Young Adult Novel in the Classroom*. Edited by Virginia Monseau and Gary Salvner. Portsmouth, NH: Boynton/Cook, 132–53, 199.

Tatum, Beverly D. *Why Are All the Black Kids Sitting Together in the Cafeteria? And Other Conversations about Race*. New York: Basic Books, 1997.

Trites, Roberta. *Disturbing the Universe: Power and Repression in Adolescent Literature*. Iowa City: University of Iowa Press, 2001.

Venkatesh, Sudhir. *American Project*. Cambridge, MA: Harvard University Press, 2000.

White, Barbra. *Growing Up Female: Adolescent Girlhood in American Fiction*. Westport, CT: Greenwood Press, 1985.

White, Shane. *Stylin': African American expressive culture from its beginnings to the zoot suit*. Ithaca: Cornell University Press, 1998.

Index

~

About the Author

Catherine Ross-Stroud is an assistant professor of language arts and literacy at Cleveland State University. She earned a Ph.D. in English at Illinois State University in Normal, Illinois. Her research is concerned with issues of adolescent identity and development. She lives in Shaker Heights, Ohio, with her daughter Lauren and their lovable dog Rupert.